STRONG IN HEART

BIBLICAL MEN
OF COMPASSION

Marjorie L. Kimbrough

DIMENSIONS
FOR LIVING
NASHVILLE

STRONG IN HEART: BIBLICAL MEN OF COMPASSION

Library of Congress Cataloging-in-Publication Data

Kimbrough, Marjorie L., 1937-
  Strong in heart : biblical men of compassion / Marjorie L. Kimbrough.
     p. cm.
  Includes bibliographical references.
  ISBN 0-687-00678-3 (binding: pbk. : alk. paper)
  1. Men in the Bible. I. Title.

  BS574.5.K56 2004
  220.9'2'081--dc22

                                                          2004010797

04 05 06 07 08 09 10 11 12 13—10 9 8 7 6 5 4 3 2 1

MANUFACTURED IN THE UNITED STATES OF AMERICA

*For my son Marty, one of the most
compassionate men I know*

Contents

Introduction

He Is Strong in Heart

*O*ne day, my son Marty came to visit me in my corporate office. I had just been informed that all but one member of the software marketing and training group I managed were moving to a new location. The young woman who was being left behind was a friend to me and my family, and she was very distressed. I promised her that I would continue to see her often and invite her to my home. I also promised that my group at work would have lunch with her, but I could not relieve her distress. She sat with her head on her desk, quietly weeping. Marty, recognizing her as a family friend, asked why she was upset. I explained the situation to him, and before he left the building he went to her office, lifted her from her chair, and gave her a big bear hug. She smiled and said that she felt so much better. Marty told me that all she really needed was a hug.

Showing compassion is often not thought of as being strong, but it is. When men are strong in heart, they have the ability to show compassion. Although the compassion they show may be mistaken for weakness or softness, it is actually a sign of true strength. Men who have the ability to show compassion are able to experience fully all of life's emotions. They know joy and sorrow and can give hugs and shed tears. Because I believe that we often fail to recognize the compassionate side of biblical men, I have chosen to direct your attention to the stories of these strong yet kindhearted men. I hope that you will be moved by their acts of compassion and will gain a new appreciation for their strength.

Esau

❧

GENESIS 33:4-11

Although Esau was the firstborn of Isaac's twin sons, we often forget about him. We remember that his brother, Jacob, stole the blessing to which he was entitled and that Jacob was the brother through whom the promise to Abraham was fulfilled. But we must also remember that Jacob had to flee from his brother, hoping to avoid his wrath. After the deception and the stolen blessing, Esau vowed to kill his brother.

But over the years that followed, God blessed both Esau and Jacob; and, although Jacob did not know it, Esau no longer wanted to kill him. Hoping to find favor with his brother, Jacob sent word of his many possessions to Esau. The messengers he sent returned with word that Esau was coming to meet him. They also reported that Esau would be accompanied by four hundred men.

When Jacob received this report, he was greatly distressed and divided his family and possessions into two groups, thinking that if one group was destroyed, the other group would escape. After praying to God for deliverance from the hand of his brother, Jacob took a gift of hundreds of animals to be given to Esau in hopes that the enormousness of the gift would assuage his brother's determination to kill him and his entire household.

But when Jacob and Esau finally met, Esau extended loving and forgiving arms around his brother, kissed him, and wept with joy. Esau asked Jacob why he had sent so many gifts ahead of him, and Jacob replied that he had much and wanted to share. Esau refused the gifts, saying that he, too, had been richly blessed by God and did not need or want anything from his brother. But Jacob insisted, noting that if he had found favor with the brother he had once deceived, he wanted Esau to accept the gifts. Jacob said, "For truly to see your face is like seeing the face of God—since you have received me with such favor" (Genesis 33:10*b*).

Just imagine. Jacob looked on the face of the brother whom he had deceived, from whom he had run away, and of whom he was afraid; and rather than seeing hate and anger, he saw the type of compassionate love and forgiveness that only God can give. Jacob thought he saw the very face of God. What a blessing!

How would you have responded if you had been Jacob? Would you have tried to find your brother? Would you have offered him gifts? Would you have anticipated his attack upon hearing that he, along with four hundred men, was coming to meet you? How would you have prepared for the attack?

What would you have done in Esau's place? Would you have accepted the gifts that were offered, or would you have killed your brother and taken all that he possessed? Would Jacob have seen the face of God when he looked into your face? Would you have had Esau's strength of heart? Would you have forgiven? Would you have offered to leave some of your company with the brother who had stolen your blessing?

Esau's story emphasizes God's abundant blessings to us all. Though your family blessing may be stolen, no one can steal your blessing from God. What God has for you is for you, and no one can deceive you and take it from you. We may not remember this hairy twin whose brother came from the womb holding on to his heel signifying that he would rule over him, but his act of forgiveness showed such strength in heart that he is surely to be counted among the biblical men of compassion.

Lord, help me have the type of forgiving heart that Esau had. Amen.

Reuben

❧

*R*euben was the firstborn of Leah's sons. In fact, as his name ("he will love me") implies, Leah believed his birth would cause Jacob to love her; but no matter how many sons Leah had, Jacob continued to love Rachel and sleep in her tent, although she was barren.

Reuben was the son who found mandrakes (a fertility-inducing fruit) and brought them to his mother. When Rachel asked for some of the mandrakes, Leah used them as leverage to get Rachel to send Jacob back to her (Leah's) tent. The mandrakes seemed to work because Rachel conceived and bore two sons. Perhaps Rachel should have thanked Reuben for finding the mandrakes, and perhaps Leah should have thanked him for Jacob's return to her tent. That return netted two additional sons and one daughter—the only daughter Jacob had.

Reuben, the firstborn, was also the son who pleaded with and finally convinced his brothers not to kill Joseph, Rachel's son and Jacob's favorite. However, without his knowledge, they agreed to sell him into slavery. Reuben came to believe that their selling Joseph into slavery and lying to their father of his death was the reason they were asked, many years later, to bring Benjamin to Egypt. Reuben knew that their father would be greatly distressed by the thought of losing the only surviving son of his beloved Rachel who had died giving birth to him. The evil they had done had caused them and their father enormous anguish.

Years later, Jacob had sent his sons, excluding Benjamin, to Egypt to purchase food during the seven years of famine. He had heard that the overseer there had great storehouses of food and supplies, but he did not know that the overseer was his long lost and presumed dead son, Joseph. When his brothers came before him to ask to buy food, Joseph recognized his brothers and demanded that Benjamin, the youngest, be brought back to him as proof that they were not spies. Joseph no doubt knew how distressed his father would be to allow Benjamin to come to him.

When the brothers returned home to Canaan—without Simeon—and told their father about the overseer's demand, Jacob refused to allow them to take Benjamin to Egypt. He even asked his sons why they had told the overseer about Benjamin in the first place. He lamented that he had already lost Joseph and now Simeon, who had been left behind at the request of the overseer. He was not willing to take the chance of also losing Benjamin.

Then Reuben showed great strength of heart as he empathized with his father. He put himself in his father's place and thought how he would feel if his sons were to be lost to him. He said, "You may kill my two sons if I do not bring him [Benjamin] back to you. Put him in my hands, and I will bring him back to you" (Genesis 42:37). Reuben probably believed that his love for his own sons equaled Jacob's love for Benjamin and Simeon, so he believed that offering the lives of his sons would guarantee for Jacob the safe return of Benjamin.

Reuben had done all that he could, but Jacob continued to refuse to let Benjamin go. It was only after their provisions had become so scarce, and it was evident that everyone in the household would die without assistance, that Jacob finally agreed. His son Judah stepped up and offered to be responsible for Benjamin, but Reuben had offered the lives of his sons. He wanted his father to know how much he understood his pain.

How would you have convinced Jacob to let Benjamin go to Egypt? What would you have done about Simeon who had been left behind? Reuben showed great strength of heart by offering the lives of his sons, for it probably was harder to contemplate sacrificing his children than to volunteer to sacrifice himself. Reuben was strong. He was a man of compassion.

Lord, strengthen me to make the sacrifices needed to show my love and devotion to thee and to those around me. Amen.

Joseph

GENESIS 50:15-21

*J*oseph was the beloved son of Jacob and Rachel. Before his birth, they had prayed for the opening of Rachel's womb. Rachel had even bargained with her sister, Leah, for some mandrakes, which were known for their fertility power. Obviously, the mandrakes worked, for Joseph was born. Even though Jacob already had ten sons, this eleventh one was most loved.

There is always a danger in showing favoritism to one child over others, and the other sons resented this favored one. After Joseph told his brothers of his dream that one day he would rule over them, they despised him even more and plotted to kill him. Eventually they decided not to kill him but rather to sell him into slavery. They deceived their father by telling him that Joseph had been killed and devoured by animals. Little did they know that God's plans for Joseph included their treacherous deeds.

Because God's hand was on Joseph, slavery was not the nightmare his brothers had intended. Everything Joseph did was blessed. He was made overseer of the house of Potiphar, his Egyptian master, and put in charge of all that he possessed. Potiphar's wife began to pursue Joseph, begging him to lie with her. But when Joseph steadfastly refused, she accused him of trying to rape her. Even the lie that she told when he refused to lie with her became a blessing. Joseph was jailed for attempted rape, but even while in jail the chief jailer put him in charge of the other prisoners.

Joseph's dream-interpreting skills proved to be the vehicle God used to free him from imprisonment. After interpreting the Pharaoh's dream, Joseph was released and put in charge of all of Egypt; only with regard to the throne was the Pharaoh greater. According to Pharaoh's dream, there would be seven years of plenty followed by seven years of famine. Joseph was charged with directing the storing of food and supplies during the years of plenty in preparation for the seven years of famine. Thus, Joseph was in the right place at the right time to save the many families that were placed under his care. He proved to be a good and compassionate leader.

During the famine, Joseph's brothers came to Egypt for food and supplies. Joseph was now in the position to provide what they needed. Joseph's brothers did not recognize him, though Joseph immediately knew who they were. Rather than refusing their request, Joseph provided them with food and also secretly returned the money they had brought for its purchase. Joseph longed to see his younger brother Benjamin, who had not traveled with his half brothers to Egypt, so he devised a plan to force his brothers to bring Benjamin back to Egypt (Genesis 42–45). Once they did, Joseph revealed himself to them. With the Pharaoh's blessings, Joseph gave his father and brothers a piece of the best land in Egypt where they could be well provided for and reunited as a family.

Jacob lived in Egypt for seventeen years before he died. After Jacob's death, the brothers feared that Joseph still held a grudge against them and, now that Jacob was dead, would seek revenge for their deeds against him. So they claimed that Jacob's dying wish was that Joseph forgive them. Joseph was so moved by their plea that he wept. He was strong enough in heart to forgive his brothers and to cause them to weep in realization of their need for forgiveness. They even promised to be his slaves. But Joseph was strong enough to know that only God could forgive them. He said, "Even though you intended to do harm to me, God intended it for good, in order to preserve a numerous people, as he is doing today" (Genesis 50:20).

Joseph certainly had the power to harm his brothers and to extract any means of vengeance he desired. Some might think that using that power would have shown his strength, but Joseph showed even greater strength by recognizing that what they had intended for evil, God intended and used for good. *Could you have been that strong? How might you have responded to this trumped-up request from a dead father? Do you think Joseph saw their fear and realized their false claim?*

Joseph had a strong and forgiving heart. He also recognized that his blessings came from God. He repeatedly claimed that he did not have the power to do anything. He was not God. God had all power. This knowledge alone made Joseph a strong biblical man of compassion.

Lord, teach me to wait for my blessings and never to give up my dreams. I know you will bless me in spite of the evil deeds and intentions of others. Amen.

Moses

EXODUS 2:11-25; DEUTERONOMY 34

*E*ven as a baby, Moses was strong. He survived being hidden by his mother for three months and survived the waters of the river before being rescued by Pharaoh's daughter. Even though he grew up in Pharaoh's house, Moses was sensitive to the forced labor and beatings the Egyptians imposed on the Hebrews. His sense of fairness and compassion led him to kill an Egyptian who had beaten a Hebrew. He even tried to stop a fight between two Hebrews and discovered that it was known that he had killed an Egyptian, so he fled to Midian.

God chose Moses to deliver the Israelites out of bondage in Egypt. God knew that Moses had the strength and compassion to accomplish the task. Moses did not believe that he could do what God assigned, but God assured him that he would provide the guidance, the power, and the words to convince Pharaoh to let the Israelites go and convince the Israelites to follow him to the promised land. God provided everything he needed. When Moses claimed that he was no speaker, God even provided him with a spokesperson.

Like so many compassionate leaders, Moses tried to do too much. He tried to be everything to everybody. He tried to settle all disputes by himself. It took his father-in-law, Jethro, to make him see that he needed help managing it all. Compassionate managers may fail to delegate responsibility, fearing that no one will be as competent and compassionate as they would be. *Have you ever had such a supervisor or known anyone with this problem?*

Moses also acted as an intercessor between the Israelites and God. He pleaded to God for help when the people complained of starving in the wilderness. God responded to their pleas by sending manna from heaven and quails for food. Moses again pleaded to the Lord on behalf of the people when they invoked God's anger by building golden images to worship. Moses urged God to "turn from your fierce wrath; change your mind and do not bring disaster on your people. . . . And the LORD changed his mind about the disaster that he planned to bring on his people" (Exodus 32:12b, 14). Moses confronted the Hebrew people regarding their sins but also asked God to forgive them. He even volunteered to be blotted out of the book God had written as atonement for the sins of the Israelites, but God assured him that only those who sinned would be punished (Exodus 32:32). Moses found favor with God, and the people were forgiven.

Moses also had to plead for the forgiveness of his sister, Miriam, who had been stricken with leprosy (Numbers 12:1-16). Miriam criticized Moses for marrying a Cushite woman rather than an Israelite and suggested that she and Aaron were also leaders through whom God had spoken. Miriam's criticisms of Moses were likely motivated by her jealousy of him and her desire for a greater role in leadership. But God became angry with Miriam, appeared in a pillar of fire, and told her that he did not speak to her the way he spoke to Moses. Though God had spoken to prophets through dreams and visions, only Moses had been allowed to see the face of God. God then struck Miriam with leprosy as punishment. Moses pleaded with God for healing on Miriam's behalf. God relented and promised that Miriam would be healed after seven days. *Would you have been compassionate enough to pray for one who wanted power equal to yours?*

Moses led the people of Israel in a way like no other: "Never since has there arisen a prophet in Israel like Moses, whom the LORD knew face to face" (Deuteronomy 34:10). He performed miraculous acts and led the people with strength, compassion, and dignity. He lived to be 120 years old and even at that age "his sight was unimpaired and his vigor had not abated" (Deuteronomy 34:7). He left his people with a spirited and wise leader, Joshua, upon whom he had laid his hands.

Would you have deserted a people who did not seem to get it after all that God had done for them? Would you have kept going to God to plead the cases of those who had sinned? Would you have chastised Aaron for letting the people run wild and build golden images? Could you have been as strong and compassionate as Moses? He was indeed strong in heart.

Lord, I want to be one through whom you communicate your laws and teach your praise. Amen.

Aaron

*W*hat *would it be like to be the spokesperson for your brother?* I can just imagine that Aaron might have wanted to be the one in charge. Why had God chosen Moses instead of him? After all, he was the older one, and he could speak without a stutter. He would have to go everywhere with Moses and repeat whatever he was told. This might have been a hard task for any of us, but it does not appear to have been hard for Aaron. The Scripture says, "[Moses and Aaron] did just as the LORD commanded them" (Exodus 7:6b). Aaron was strong in heart; he was not concerned about who got the credit or who was the leader. He just wanted to do what the Lord commanded.

I believe that Aaron's wanting to do what the Lord commanded caused him to become angry with Moses and speak against him when Moses married a Cushite woman. Aaron probably considered it a sin to marry someone who was not a Hebrew and therefore did not worship God. So he joined with their sister, Miriam, and raised the questions, "Has the LORD spoken only through Moses? Has he not spoken through us also?" (Numbers 12:2). But God was not pleased with their questions and made it clear to them that he did not speak to them the same way he spoke to Moses. God said, "With him I speak face to face—clearly, not in riddles; and he beholds the form of the LORD. Why then were you not afraid to speak against my servant Moses?" (Numbers 12:8). I am sure that God's words brought Aaron back to reality, and he remembered his position in relation to Moses. He was to assist; he was not to take the lead. God did not speak to him face-to-face. In all likelihood, he was ashamed of the anger he had expressed.

It appears to me that Miriam was the one who really wanted position as a prophet. I believe that she talked Aaron into raising the questions about Moses because when God demonstrated his displeasure with the two of them, Miriam was the only one punished with leprosy. Aaron could have turned his back on Miriam. After all, he was not affected, but he immediately turned to Moses and begged him to ask God not to punish them for such a foolish sin. He admitted that they both had sinned and seeing his sister suffer was punishment enough for him. He had compassion and begged his brother to have compassion. *Would you have been strong enough to ask this of a brother toward whom you had evidenced some jealousy? What would be your plan if he refused to help? Would you be prepared to apologize for your sinfulness?*

Moses did not deny Aaron's request and pleaded to God for mercy and healing. Eventually God did heal Miriam, but she had seven days to think over her sin and desire for power. After the seven days had passed, the leprosy disappeared.

Because of his concern and compassion for the people who wanted something tangible to worship, Aaron allowed the people to build golden images. He knew that the people wanted a god they could see and touch and feel, and he probably did not know that he was doing anything wrong. Moses had to set him straight. I don't believe he intended to respond sinfully; he simply tried to respond to the people's need. *What would you have done with a group of people begging for a god to worship?* Aaron must have proved himself to be worthy, for he and his sons were given responsibility for the offenses connected with the sanctuary and were put in charge of the offerings and holy gifts made to God (Numbers 18:1). Aaron, along with his sons and daughters, was given a priestly portion of all that was given to God in perpetuity (Numbers 18:11). *Would God have entrusted him and his heirs with such great responsibility or have been so generous to him if he had not been a strong man of compassion?* I don't think so.

Lord, I, like Aaron, often stray from your will. Lead me back to your holy sanctuary. Amen.

Jethro

EXODUS 18:13-23

*J*ethro, the priest of Midian, was Moses' father-in-law. He offered Moses sound advice because he had compassion for Moses and saw that what Moses was doing would soon wear him out.

Jethro knew that Moses had been chosen by God to deliver the Hebrews from bondage in Egypt. He also knew that Moses was one to whom God spoke. He must have seen Moses' dedication to duty and willingness to offer counsel to the people for whom he felt responsible. He noticed that Moses was working from morning until evening, and he asked Moses what he was doing. Moses explained that he was telling the people what God wanted them to do and how to settle their disputes. Although Jethro did not question Moses' ability to sit as judge for the people, he did question his act of sitting in judgment alone. It was obvious to him that Moses needed help.

Others might not have cared that Moses was wearing himself out, but Jethro did. He knew that Moses would not endure if he continued his leadership tasks at the same pace. The burden was too heavy for one man alone. So Jethro offered advice. He told Moses to teach the people God's statutes and instructions. He wanted Moses to let the people know the way they should live and the things they should do. He could not continue to be the only one with the knowledge God had given him.

Jethro also advised Moses to look for trustworthy and God-fearing men among the people who could serve as officers over various groups of people. These officers could hear and settle some of the cases that the people brought, and only the more difficult cases would have to be brought to Moses. Because he cared, Jethro taught Moses how to distribute the workload.

I wonder how compassionate we are. *Do we care that our leaders are overworked and worn out? Do we ever volunteer to help with the workload, or are we among the ones who insist that the pastor or the boss is the only one who can handle our situation?*

Jethro was a wise and compassionate priest. He appreciated the relationship that Moses had with God and knew that Moses was doing a good job, but he also realized that Moses would soon be of no use to God if he wore himself out. *How many of us know that? Do we need Jethro to remind us that we need to divide the workload rather than try to do it all ourselves?*

Jethro was strong enough in heart to offer compassionate advice. Thank God that Moses was wise enough to accept it. I wonder if we are.

God, keep me from overloading myself with day-to-day responsibilities. Help me trust others to share the load. Amen.

Joshua

*J*oshua was obviously a strong man because Moses chose him to be the new leader. *Have you ever been chosen to succeed a great leader? How did you feel? Did you believe you could live up to the expectations? Did the people you were to lead respect your leadership, or did they still long for their previous leader? Did they agree to follow your direction?* I am sure that Joshua must have asked himself these questions many times, but the scripture says that "Moses had laid his hands on him; and the Israelites obeyed him, doing as the LORD had commanded Moses" (Deuteronomy 34:9*b*).

What was it about Joshua that God revealed to Moses? Did Moses see wisdom, courage, compassion, and strength? Did he see obedience to God's commandments and the ability to lead God's people? These were qualities that Moses certainly had. Moses must have known that God would speak directly to Joshua just the way God had spoken directly to him. And God did speak to Joshua and promised to be with him every step of the way. That knowledge alone would have made Joshua strong. *But how was he compassionate?*

Joshua was a brilliant military leader. He led successful

campaigns against the Canaanites, and the Israelite tribes were able to establish a just and free society in the land that God had given them. We know that Joshua spared Rahab, the prostitute, and all of her family. She had helped the men Joshua sent to spy out the land by hiding them from the King of Jericho (Joshua 2:1-21). She and her family did not perish with the rest of the town when Joshua and the Israelites conquered Jericho (Joshua 6:17).

But Joshua's accomplishments were not limited to battle. He became a strong leader. After leading the Israelites in the conquest of several cities on the west side of the Jordan, he oversaw the dividing of the promised land among the tribes, though most of it had not yet been conquered. Many years later when he was old, he addressed the nation, reminding them of all that God had done for them and urging their continued obedience and faithfulness. He challenged them to choose the one they would serve while he boldly announced that he and his house would worship God. He knew that they could have not conquered any of the land without God and only through their continued and undivided devotion to God would the land promised as their inheritance be completely conquered. He warned them of the price of their disobedience and urged them to renew their commitment and devotion to God. Like Moses, Joshua had in the past pleaded with the Lord to spare the people when some disobeyed God's commands and stole things devoted to other gods during the conquest of Jericho (Joshua 7). Joshua had to weed out those at fault so that all of Israel could be spared. He did not want Israel to perish because of the selfish deeds of a few. What an awesome responsibility! *Have you ever had to separate the innocent from the guilty?* Surely Joshua knew what it meant to be strong and yet compassionate. *Do you?*

Lord, I want to be like Joshua by leading those around me to choose to serve you. Amen.

Boaz

RUTH 2–4

*A*lthough he did not have to, Boaz showed compassion to Ruth, a beautiful, hardworking, loyal young widow. Perhaps it was providential that Ruth, who had come to Judah with her mother-in-law to find food, went to his field to glean. According to Israelite law, the poor were allowed to gather food left in the fields after the reapers had finished their work. She did not know the field belonged to Boaz or that he was related to her late father-in-law. Ruth went to the fields to provide for herself and her mother-in-law, Naomi. She did not know that she would be noticed and then provided for.

Boaz noticed Ruth as soon as he came to his fields. He wanted to know who she was and to whom she belonged, believing her to be a servant. But he was informed that she was the woman who had accompanied Naomi from Moab and had asked to glean behind the reapers. The report was that she had faithfully worked all day without taking a break. Boaz was also impressed by the loyalty Ruth had shown to her mother-in-law, having left her homeland and her people to come to a foreign place.

He invited Ruth to glean only in his fields, and extended

his bread and wine to her during mealtime. He also instructed his men to let her glean even among the standing sheaves and to pull out some handfuls for her from the bundles (Ruth 2:15-16). He assumed the role of provider and protector. Although his actions may have indicated that he was interested in her personally, he did act with great compassion.

Boaz took the time to find out about Ruth and the loyalty she had shown to her mother-in-law. He felt that her compassion and kindness should be rewarded. He knew that she had left her homeland and her people and had come to a foreign place. He comforted her with his kindness. He made sure that she had more than enough for herself and Naomi. *Would you have been as generous as Boaz?*

At the end of the harvests, Naomi encouraged Ruth to anoint and adorn herself and go to Boaz and lie down at his feet on the threshing floor. As was the case in that culture, marriage was really the only option for a woman's survival. So Naomi saw Ruth's marriage to Boaz as the way to provide security for both of them. According to Israelite law, if a married man died, it was the responsibility of his brother or next of kin to marry his widow and thus provide for her.

Boaz welcomed Ruth to lie with him and admitted that although he was not her next of kin, he would assume that role if no one else did. Until the other kinsman could be consulted and the matter settled, Boaz took care not to have Ruth return to her mother-in-law empty-handed and gave her a large quantity of barley. Again, this was something he did not have to do, but it clearly showed that Boaz was also concerned for both Naomi's and Ruth's welfare and wanted to provide for them no matter how things turned out. *How would you have responded to this beautiful, young widow? Would you have given her anything? Would you have taken advantage of her? Would you have offered to marry her?*

Boaz continued to show compassion for Ruth by presenting the rights to the land that had belonged to her father-in-law to the person who was next of kin. He knew that Ruth went along with the land, but he could not marry her or retain the land in the name of her late husband without the consent of the next of kin. Because of his wealth, Boaz might have been able to usurp the rights of the next of kin, but he did not. He wanted his relationship with Ruth to be legal. *If you had been Boaz, how would you have handled this next-of-kin situation?* Boaz was strong enough to give Ruth up if that was the right thing to do. *Would you have been that strong?* God intervened and a favorable agreement was reached when all of the facts were presented to the next of kin, and Boaz married Ruth. Their marriage produced a son, Obed, who became the father of Jesse who, in turn, became the father of David. God was always in the plan of Boaz's compassion.

God, help me learn from the compassionate spirit of Boaz and willingly provide for the care of those who depend on me. Amen.

Samuel

1 SAMUEL 3:1-10

*I*f ever a child was truly desired and prayed for, it was Samuel. His mother, Hannah, had wept and fasted because she was so ashamed of her barrenness. She had faced ridicule from Peninnah, her husband's other wife who had been blessed with children. Hannah had prayed so fervently for a child that the priest, Eli, accused her of being drunk and making a public spectacle of herself. She asked God for a loving and compassionate son whom she vowed to present to the temple to be raised by the priest and given back to God.

That much prayed-for child, Samuel, was born and, when he was weaned, was presented to God to be raised in the temple by Eli. But his mother did not abandon him; she returned to visit with him and made him a new coat every year. That child grew "both in stature and in favor with the LORD and with the people" (1 Samuel 2:26*b*). I am sure that Samuel was of great comfort to the aging Eli whose own sons "were scoundrels [and] had no regard for the LORD" (1 Samuel 2:12). At least someone for whom he had responsibility was God-fearing. *Can you relate to the way Eli must have felt about Samuel and about his own sons?*

Samuel was an obedient and sensitive child. He ministered to the Lord under Eli, and when he heard the voice of God as he lay in the temple, he immediately responded and ran to Eli. But Eli had not called Samuel and told him to go back and lie down. After three such trips, Eli realized that it must be God who was calling Samuel and instructed him to respond to the call, if he should hear it again, by saying, "Speak, LORD, for your servant is listening" (1 Samuel 3:9b). Samuel did as he was told.

God had chosen Samuel to be a prophet to the people and revealed through Samuel his visions concerning the house of Eli and the future of Israel. Although the kind and compassionate Samuel was afraid to tell Eli what God had said, Eli compelled him. *How would you have felt about giving Eli a bad report?* God continued to work through Samuel, and all Israel knew that he was "a trustworthy prophet of the LORD" (1 Samuel 3:20b).

One would have to be strong to be separated from a loving mother, and Samuel was strong. One would have to have compassion for an aging priest who had been a father figure, and Samuel showed compassion to Eli. Samuel knew the fate that awaited the house of Eli, but he remained strong and devoted to God. Samuel grew in his role as prophet, and all who came in contact with him knew that he had been called of God. When the Israelites started worshiping foreign gods, Samuel encouraged them to return to the Lord with all of their hearts. When the Israelites obeyed his urgings, they were successful in battle and immeasurably blessed by God.

When Samuel grew old and it was clear that his sons, who had been appointed judges of the people, were corrupt and not blessed with his wisdom, the Israelites asked for a king to rule over them. This request made Samuel unhappy, but when he prayed to God about the people's request, God told him to listen to the people. God pointed out to Samuel that the people were in fact rejecting God, not him.

Even in his old age, Samuel was attentive and obedient to the counsel of God, and he anointed Saul as king. Eventually Samuel regretted that Saul had ever been anointed, for Saul disobeyed God's commandment and, because of this, Samuel grieved mightily. But God asked him how long he would grieve over a king who had failed and instructed him to take his horn of oil and anoint a new king. Again, in obedience, Samuel took his oil and anointed David, the king whose heart and spirit were of God.

When Samuel completed his work, I can imagine that he reviewed all of the obstacles he had faced. He had been separated from his loving family. *How would you have dealt with that?* Samuel had been called by God for a special mission and had to tell Eli, who had raised him and was his father figure, that his sons were corrupt and that an unfavorable fate awaited them. *Could you have done that?* He had to recognize the unfaithfulness of his own sons and respond to God's call to find and anoint a new leader. *Have you ever had to admit to the unfaithfulness of a family member?* He grieved over the first king he anointed, and God had to tell him to get over it and move on. *Have you ever had to get over something or someone and move on?*

Samuel successfully finished his course, anointed a new king, and demonstrated compassion in his dealings with others. He had proved to be a strong man of God. *What about you?*

God, teach me to listen for and respond to your call. Amen.

David

1 SAMUEL 25; 2 SAMUEL 9, 18

*T*here are at least three instances in which I believe David demonstrated strength of heart and great compassion. The first instance involved Abigail, the wife of Nabal. Nabal was a rich property owner in Carmel, and David and his men had watched over and protected Nabal's men and his sheep. When the time for shearing came, David expected that he and his men would be invited to participate in the food and festivities that accompanied shearing. But Nabal refused, and David was angry.

David decided to kill Nabal and his entire household. However, when the beautiful and clever Abigail was told of this insult to the future king of all of Israel, she quickly prepared food and drink for David and his men. She apologized for Nabal and reminded David that he would one day become king and therefore would not want the blood of a fool such as Nabal on his hands. She actually helped David understand his mission and ministry, which, in turn, strengthened his heart.

David had the good sense and compassion to accept the apology and listen to Abigail who also asked him to remember her when he became king. When Nabal learned that his wife had saved all of their lives and that he had insulted the future king, he had a stroke (and perhaps a heart attack) and died (1 Samuel 25:37-38). David remembered Abigail's request. He could have forgotten that she had helped him understand his mission and he could have forgotten that she had asked to be remembered when he became king. But when he learned that she was widowed, he showed compassion by remembering her and honoring her request. His heart had been both touched and strengthened by this beautiful woman, and he asked her to become his wife. *How would you have remembered Abigail? What could David have offered besides marriage? Was Abigail asking for marriage when she asked to be remembered?*

The second instance I have chosen to lift up occurred after David became king. David remembered his boyhood friend, Jonathan, and wanted to show kindness to anyone left of the house of Saul for Jonathan's sake. Again, David did not have to do it, but his strong and compassionate heart prevailed. After the death of both Saul and Jonathan, Ziba, one of the servants of the house of Saul, told David about Jonathan's crippled son, Mephibosheth, and David sent for him. Upon meeting with Mephibosheth, David said, "I will restore to you all the land of your grandfather Saul, and you yourself shall eat at my table always" (2 Samuel 9:7*b*). From that time forward, Mephibosheth ate at David's table just like one of the king's sons. Mephibosheth was blessed with land, produce, and servants for the rest of his life.

Why do you think David wanted to do something for Jonathan's family? Do you think that David felt that all or at least some of what he inherited as king really should have remained with the house of Saul? What is the significance of inviting someone to eat at your table? Would you invite your enemy's grandson to your table?

The third instance involved David's son Absalom. Absalom is described as very handsome. "Now in all Israel there was no one to be praised so much for his beauty as

Absalom; from the sole of his foot to the crown of his head there was no blemish in him" (2 Samuel 14:25). David truly loved this beautiful son.

Absalom fled in fear after killing his brother Amnon as revenge for the rape of Tamar, their sister, and lived in exile for three years. As a result, David had lost his sons Amnon and Absalom. David decided to bring Absalom home and work to restore their relationship. *Why do you think this restoration was important to David? Would it have been important to you?*

Though David was interested in reestablishing a peaceful and loving relationship with his son, Absalom had ambitions of his own. He plotted against his father and sought to become king over Israel. When David learned of this plot, he fled Jerusalem before Absalom and his men could reach the city. David gathered his army, and they prepared for war against Absalom and his troops. In spite of Absalom's treachery against him, David asked his men to spare the life of his son during the battle. David showed great compassion for one who sought to kill him.

When Absalom was killed, two runners came to report to David. Somehow David knew that they brought good news about the victory of his troops in battle. Although he felt certain that they had stopped Absalom's troops, David's main concern was Absalom. The first runner said that he did not know Absalom's fate, but the second runner reported, "May the enemies of my lord the king, and all who rise up to do you harm, be like that young man" (2 Samuel 18:32*b*). This report moved David to tears.

David, the strong and valiant warrior, wept for his son, saying, "O my son Absalom, my son, my son Absalom! Would I had died instead of you, O Absalom, my son, my son!" (2 Samuel 18:33*b*). David knew that this son sought to overthrow him; yet, still he wept for him and wished that he could have died in his place. *Would you have been that compassionate?*

David remembered past kindnesses. *Do you remember those who have been kind to you?* He remembered that Abigail had kept him from unnecessary bloodshed and he remembered his love for Jonathan and his early encounters with King Saul. *Do you, like David, remember to say thank-you even to a relative of one you love?* David remembered a beautiful and brave son—even a son who would have killed him and all of his men. *What would you have done? Would you have grieved for Absalom?* David was in every sense a strong man, but he was also a man of great compassion.

Lord, you said that David was a person after your own heart. I want you to be able to say that of me. Amen.

The Men of Jabesh-gilead

*I*n what would be his final battle, Saul led the Israelites against the Philistine army, but Saul's men were forced to flee before the powerful army. The army overtook Saul and his sons. Their backs were against the wall. Saul's sons were killed, and he was wounded. Not wanting to die at the hands of the enemy the way his sons had, Saul asked his armor-bearer to kill him. The armor-bearer was too terrified to take his master's life, so Saul fell upon his own sword and died. Then the armor-bearer fell upon his sword. Saul, his sons, and his armor-bearer all died on the same day.

Knowing that Saul was dead, the company of Israel fled, and the Philistines occupied their towns. Then they stripped Saul's body, cut off his head, placed his armor in the temple of Astarte, and nailed his body to the wall of Bethshan. But when the people of Jabesh-gilead heard what had been done to Saul, some valiant men rode all night and took Saul's body off the wall.

These valiant men could not allow such disgrace to befall the former king of Israel. They could not even allow such disgrace to his sons. They had too much respect for the position Saul had held. After all, he had liberated their city from the rule of the Ammonites and had been their king. They remembered his past accomplishments and felt that he deserved a proper burial and period of mourning. They were strong and valiant men of great compassion.

These strong men teach us many lessons. They teach us that although others desert us and use and abuse our bodies, there are still some who will love and respect us. God always sends someone to rescue us and "take us off the wall." These valiant men also teach us to respect our leaders and to show them the simple courtesies their offices deserve. They teach us to observe religious burials and mourn for the departed. They were strong and compassionate men.

What would you have done for Saul and his sons? Would you have risked going into enemy territory to get them off the wall and see to their proper burial? Would you have had sufficient respect for the office Saul had held and the good he had accomplished? Would you have mourned for him? Are you strong enough in heart? Do you have great compassion for others? The men of Jabesh-gilead did.

Lord, teach me respect for those in authority and compassion for those in need. Amen.

Solomon

———————

❧

1 KINGS 3:1-15

Solomon was the beloved son of David and Bathsheba.
He reigned as king after his father, and he was blessed and
allowed to build God's temple. Although it appeared that
Solomon had everything he could ever want, he felt inade-
quate to rule over and govern God's people. He cried to
God, "And now, O LORD my God, you have made your servant king in place of my father David, although I am only a
little child; I do not know how to go out or come in"
(1 Kings 3:7).

Solomon felt overwhelmed by the enormousness of the
task he faced. He recognized that he did not have the wisdom to govern fairly and efficiently. He had probably prayed
mightily over this matter, and God appeared to him in a
dream, asking him what God could give him. Solomon
answered, "Give your servant therefore an understanding
mind to govern your people, able to discern between good
and evil; for who can govern this your great people?"
(1 Kings 3:9).

Solomon showed great compassion for God's people by
asking for the wisdom to govern them with righteousness. He
asked for an understanding mind so that he would know the

concerns of the people and be able to make the best decisions for them and the right decisions according to God's statutes. He could have asked for long life, good health, riches, or revenge on his enemies, but these would not have been compassionate requests. Yet, because he did not ask for these, God gave him wisdom and riches and honor all of his life.

God promised that there would never be another king like Solomon—no one would be able to measure up to his standards. Solomon demonstrated the great wisdom God had given him in settling a dispute over a child between two women. Both women lived in the same house and had recently given birth to children. However, one of the children died when his mother accidentally smothered him. When she realized that her child was dead, she switched her dead child with the living child of the other woman during the night. But in the morning, the second woman realized that the dead child in her bed was not her son. Since both women claimed that the living child was hers, they went to the king to resolve the argument. Solomon listened to the dispute and threatened to divide the child in half so that both women claiming to be its mother could have a part of the child. Of course, the real mother could not allow her child to be killed, so she begged Solomon to give the child to the other woman rather than see him killed (1 Kings 3:16-28). Solomon realized at once that this woman was the child's true mother and returned the child to her.

How might you have handled that dispute? I wonder how many of us would have been wise enough or brave enough to think of the solution Solomon did. This illustration also directs us to Solomon's compassionate nature. Only one who really understands love and care could anticipate such a loving response. As long as Solomon continued to walk in God's way, keeping his commandments and statutes, God would fulfill the promise to grant Solomon wisdom, long life, and prosperity. Solomon was equal to the task, and he was granted long life as well.

If you had inherited a kingdom and built a great temple, what would you have asked for? Would you have recognized your inexperience? Would you have sought protection from your enemies? Would you have desired unending wealth and riches? Or would you have been wise enough or compassionate enough to ask for something that would greatly benefit others? Solomon put the welfare of God's people before any concern of his own. He truly wanted to be a good, fair, and compassionate ruler. *What kind of leader, parent, spouse, or family member do you want to be?*

God, I need the wisdom of Solomon as I face my daily trials. Amen.

Obadiah

1 Kings 18:1-16

*O*badiah was the chief steward in charge of the palace of King Ahab. Ahab had married Jezebel, a foreign princess, under whose influence he began worshiping the Canaanite god, Baal.

Although Obadiah was a reverent, God-fearing man, he was afraid openly to defy the king and his wicked wife, Jezebel. But in secret, he "took a hundred prophets, hid them fifty to a cave, and provided them with bread and water" (1 Kings 18:4*b*). He was so full of compassion that he could not stand by while Jezebel killed off the prophets of the Lord. Just think, although Obadiah was afraid of the consequences, he devised a plan to save a hundred prophets of the Lord. No one told him to do it, and he could not guarantee either his own safety or that of the prophets. But he cared enough to try and was successful. *What would you have done in Obadiah's place? Would you have been afraid of Ahab and Jezebel?*

During the third year of the drought that had engulfed the land, Ahab told Obadiah to help him search for water and grass so that some of the animals might be saved. Ahab and Obadiah divided the land between them and set out in different directions. While he was on his search, Obadiah met the prophet Elijah who instructed him to tell the king of Elijah's presence. But Obadiah was afraid to tell the king, believing that the king would kill him for delivering such news. King Ahab had looked everywhere for Elijah but had been unable to find him. Every time Elijah was reported as having been seen, he would disappear before Ahab could capture him. So Obadiah feared that the same thing would happen when he reported the whereabouts of Elijah. He knew that it was possible that the Spirit of God could carry Elijah away, and Ahab would be so angry that he would kill Obadiah. *How would you have responded to Elijah's request? Would you have reminded him that you had already saved a hundred prophets of the Lord? Would you have believed that you had done enough?*

Elijah convinced Obadiah that he would appear before Ahab that very day, so Obadiah agreed to tell Ahab where Elijah was. When Elijah and Ahab met, Elijah demonstrated the miraculous power of God against the power of Baal and his 450 prophets (1 Kings 18:20-40). This very demonstration might not have been possible if Obadiah had not conquered his fears and brought the two together. Obadiah was compassionate, courageous, and God-fearing. He risked his own life to save a hundred of God's prophets and to lead Ahab to Elijah. He was strong in heart.

Lord, sometimes I am afraid to do what I am told. Help me discern right from wrong and know that you are with me if I act according to your will. Amen.

Elisha

‿‿

2 KINGS 2:1-15

W*ho is the most spiritually connected person you know? Who has the closest relationship with God? Whose spirit do you want to emulate? Are you brave enough to ask for a double portion of that person's spirit?* Elisha was.

Elisha must have wanted to be in a position to demonstrate God's great power. He had observed his mentor, Elijah, and knew that through God it was possible to raise the dead, heal the sick, part the waters of the Jordan, and perform other miracles that relieved suffering and brought people closer to God.

During their last journey together before Elijah was to be taken away, he repeatedly told Elisha to stay behind, but Elisha ignored his wishes. Elisha wanted to be with Elijah. He really wanted to hang on to him as long as he could. Perhaps Elisha felt that he had not learned enough and was not ready to proceed on his own. So Elisha vowed not to leave Elijah until he was taken away to be with God.

First, Elisha followed Elijah to Bethel, the place of worship. It might have been comfortable for Elisha to stay there, but when Elijah moved on, so did he. Then they continued on to Jericho, the place where the walls had been torn down.

That might have been a place representing spiritual warfare and surely Elisha would not want to stay there. Finally, he followed Elijah across the river Jordan, the place of earthly death but also of heavenly beginnings. Jordan was to be the place about which the company of prophets had warned him. Several times they had told him that his master would be taken away, but he ignored and silenced their warnings. When Elijah saw that Elisha was determined to be with him, Elijah asked what Elisha wanted him to do before his time of departure came. Elisha boldly asked for a double share of Elijah's spirit. Just think what Elisha could do for God if he had twice as much spirit as his mentor had.

Of course, Elijah granted the wish contingent on Elisha's being present to see him leave. Elisha must have stuck to Elijah like glue because he was right there when Elijah ascended into heaven in a whirlwind. After compassionately calling Elijah, "Father, Father," and no longer being able to see Elijah, Elisha picked up the mantle that had fallen from Elijah and struck the Jordan in much the same manner that Elijah had. Again, the waters parted and the company of prophets recognized that the spirit of Elijah now rested on Elisha.

But it was not just the spirit of Elijah; it was twice the spirit of Elijah. Elisha would be able to do far greater works than those of his mentor. The authority of Elijah had been transferred to Elisha. As a prophet of God, Elisha had been given the power to perform miraculous deeds in God's name. Elisha made it possible for a widow to pay off all of her husband's debts by seeing that she had an inexhaustible supply of oil (2 Kings 4:1-7); he raised the Shunammite woman's son from the dead (2 Kings 4:18-36); and he cured Naaman's leprosy, and everyone knew that there was a prophet in Israel (2 Kings 5:1-19).

Yes, Elisha was strong in heart. He was a man of great compassion and wanted everyone to know of the power and majesty of God. *Do you want everyone to know how great your God is? Do you have the compassion of Elisha that would not allow a widow to sell her sons to pay her debts or a woman who was barren to lose the son she loved or an unbeliever to go through life with a dreaded disease?* Elisha was prepared; he asked for a double portion of God's spirit. *How much are you asking for?*

Lord, equip me with a double portion of your spirit so that I may serve you doubly well. Amen.

Naaman's Servants

2 KINGS 5:1-14

*N*aaman's servants knew he was ill. He was suffering from the dreaded disease leprosy. Even though Naaman was commander of the army of the king of Aram and a mighty and powerful warrior, he had no power to cure himself.

When the Hebrew servant girl who attended Naaman's wife suggested that Naaman go to see the prophet in Samaria who had the power to cure leprosy, Naaman went to his king to ask permission to go to Israel. Not knowing that the king of Israel had nothing to do with the prophet's power, the king of Aram composed a letter to the king of Israel requesting that he cure Naaman. Relations between their country and Israel had been rocky and filled with conflict, so Naaman realized that he would need to go through official diplomatic channels to gain an audience with Elisha. Along with the letter Naaman carried silver, gold, and garments as gifts for the king in appreciation of the cure that was sure to occur. But the king of Israel misunderstood the intention of the letter, suspecting the Israelites of trying to pick a quarrel by making what seemed an impossible request of him. The king of Israel became so angry that he tore his clothes and said, "Am I God, to give death or life, that this

man sends word to me to cure a man of his leprosy?"
(2 Kings 5:7*b*).

Elisha, the prophet, heard of the king's distress and sent a
message to the king requesting that Naaman be sent to him
so that he would learn that there really was a prophet in
Israel. Naaman and his servants traveled to Elisha's house,
but when they arrived, Elisha did not even come out to speak
to them. Instead, he sent word to have Naaman go wash in
the Jordan River seven times and he would be cured.

Naaman was greatly insulted that Elisha did not bother to
come out and address him personally and call on his God
and touch him or wave his hand over him. He questioned
whether the rivers in his own land were not as good as the
river Jordan. He did not understand why it was necessary for
him to make the journey to do something as simple and
meaningless as to wash seven times in the Jordan. Naaman
left Elisha's house in a rage.

But his servants, who had compassion for him, reasoned
with him by saying, "Father, if the prophet had commanded
you to do something difficult, would you not have done it?
How much more, when all he said to you was, 'Wash, and be
clean'?" (2 Kings 5:13*b*). Naaman listened to his servants,
knowing that they cared about him and wanted him to be
cured. He decided that he would follow the instructions he
had been given and immersed himself in the Jordan seven
times. All were amazed that not only was his leprosy cured,
but also his flesh was like the flesh of a young boy.

*How do you think Naaman felt when he discovered that
he had been cured? Do you think he thanked his servants
for insisting that he follow the prophet's orders? Do you
think he regretted not having believed in the first place? Do
you think he understood why Elisha had not personally
addressed him?*

Naaman and his servants returned to Elisha's house and
thanked him personally for the cure. Naaman had witnessed
the power of the God of Israel and declared to Elisha, "Now

I know that there is no God in all the earth except in Israel"
(2 Kings 5:15). Just think what a blessing Naaman would
have missed had it not been for the compassionate insistence
and reasoning of his servants. Because of their heartfelt concern, Naaman came to know the God of Israel. *Look around
you; is there someone you can reason with and introduce to
the God of Israel?*

*God, bless me to respond to the simple instructions of life,
for by responding, I may lead someone to you. Amen.*

Asa

1 KINGS 15:9-24; 2 CHRONICLES 14:8-13

*A*sa was the fourth king of Judah. The united monarchy was divided by civil war after the death of Solomon, and the kingdom had been divided into two kingdoms—Judah in the south and Israel in the north. Asa was a good king and did what he could to restore Judah to worship the God of their ancestors. He expelled the male temple prostitutes from the land. He removed foreign incense altars and idols his ancestors had made and commanded that all in Judah seek the Lord and keep God's law. He led Judah in building cities, and the inhabitants of those cities prospered in peace.

But the peaceful period did not last, for Zerah the Ethiopian marched against Judah. Although Asa was willing to go to battle with thousands of troops, his enemy, Zerah, had an army of a million. Asa knew that he was greatly outnumbered and realized that they would prevail only by reliance on the power of God, and he did not want anyone to claim that a warrior who relied on God had been defeated. He was a tough warrior, ready to fight, but there was also tenderness in his toughness. The scripture does not say that he prayed to God; it says that he cried to the Lord, his God, for aid. His cry was, "O LORD, there is no difference for you between helping the mighty and the weak. Help us, O LORD our God, for we rely on you, and in your name we have come against this multitude. O LORD, you are our God; let no mortal prevail against you" (2 Chronicles 14:11).

Asa knew that he had done all he could to help Judah return to God. He had lived with his people in peace. He must have wondered why this Ethiopian had come out against him. *Why is it that even when you try to live in peace, the enemy may still attack? How do you respond to such attacks?*

Asa was a great warrior, but he did not want to fight. He was a compassionate man, so he cried to the Lord. He had the strength of heart and humility to know that he could not rely simply on his own efforts. *Would you have cried to the Lord for help, or would your pride and sense of self-reliance have caused you to rush headlong into battle?* Asa pleaded for assistance against the enemy. He pleaded not only for his own reputation and victory, but also for God's reputation and victory. *What would you have done? Do you care about your reputation? Do you care about God's reputation?* Asa did not want any mortal to prevail against the God he served and knew to be a mighty God. He was a king of compassion. *What about you?*

God, help me know how to respond when the enemy attacks. Amen.

Jehoiada

❧

2 Chronicles 22:10–24:16

*J*ehoiada was known as a good priest. He was married to Jehoshabeath, the daughter of King Jehoram of Judah. King Jehoram was a wicked king who was married to Athaliah, the wicked daughter of Jezebel. When Jehoram died, his son, Ahaziah, assumed the throne but, under the influence of his mother, Athaliah, he followed "in the ways of the house of Ahab." In other words, Ahaziah engaged in and sanctioned the worship of foreign gods. After ruling for only a year, Ahaziah was killed, leaving no one of the house of Judah to rule. Ahaziah's wicked mother, Athaliah, seized control of the throne. To secure her position, Athaliah ordered the execution of all of the other members of the royal family so there would be no one to challenge her. *Can you imagine someone ordering the execution of her family members— even her own grandchildren? Have you ever wanted power that badly? Do you know of anyone who would kill for power? How does the lure of power tend to corrupt those who seek it?*

Hearing of her stepmother's plan, Jehoshabeath hid her youngest nephew, Ahaziah's baby son, in a palace bedroom and later took him home with her so he would not be killed.

She and her husband, Jehoiada, raised that child, Joash, until he was seven years old. They actually hid the child in the house of the Lord while Athaliah reigned on the throne. Jehoiada was able to instruct the child in the laws of God and to help his wife preserve the lineage of David. If Athaliah had been successful in her mission to kill all of her grandchildren, there would have been no one of the line of David ever again to assume the throne. *Do you think God would have allowed that to happen? What would have happened to the ancestry of the expected Messiah?*

When Jehoiada felt that the time was right, he courageously presented Joash to the people and announced that Athaliah had no claim to the throne. Jehoiada said, "Here is the king's son! Let him reign, as the LORD promised concerning the sons of David" (2 Chronicles 23:3*b*). Jehoiada set up guards for Joash and crowned him while the people shouted, "Long live the king!" When Athaliah heard the commotion, she claimed treason, but Jehoiada had her brought out of the house of the Lord and put to death. *Why do you think it was necessary to kill Athaliah? Do you think that Joash at seven years old was old enough to assume the throne?*

After Joash assumed the throne, Jehoiada renewed the covenant among the Lord and the king and the people reminding them that they would be the Lord's people. They tore down the house of Baal and restored the house of the Lord. It was written, "Joash did what was right in the sight of the LORD all the days of the priest Jehoiada" (2 Chronicles 24:2). Unfortunately, after Jehoiada's death, Joash listened to some of the officials of Judah and was persuaded to abandon the worship of God. Although Jehoiada could not guarantee that Joash would always serve God, he did make certain that Joash obeyed God's commandments during his lifetime. I am sure that many parents would be proud if their children would live their lives in accordance with the laws of God at least during the parents' lifetime. *Why do you think it is so hard to remain faithful after the death of one who has worked to keep you in righteous living?* It is good that Jehoiada did not know what happened to Joash after his death, for he was a good priest and a strong man of compassion. He died knowing that he helped save and raise a baby who preserved the throne of David.

Lord, give me the wisdom to know when to accept responsibility for your endangered children. Amen.

Hezekiah

❦

2 KINGS 18–20; 2 CHRONICLES 29–33; ISAIAH 36–39

*H*ezekiah was such a good king that it was said of him, "There was no one like him among all the kings of Judah after him, or among those who were before him. For he held fast to the LORD; he did not depart from following him but kept the commandments that the LORD commanded Moses. The LORD was with him; wherever he went, he prospered" (2 Kings 18:5*b*-7*a*). During the first year of his reign, Hezekiah repaired the temple in Jerusalem and told the priests and the Levites to sanctify both themselves and the house of the Lord. He told them to carry out the filth from God's holy place and to reject the unfaithfulness of their ancestors. I wonder how many of us would have been strong enough to assume command of a nation and challenge the religious leaders to clean up their act. Hezekiah was that strong.

Hezekiah said, "Now it is in my heart to make a covenant with the LORD, the God of Israel, so that his fierce anger may turn away from us. My sons, do not now be negligent, for the LORD has chosen you to stand in his presence to minister to him, and to be his ministers and make offerings to him" (2 Chronicles 29:10-11). His very words tell us how strong in heart and compassionate he was. *Do we ever hear the call to minister to the Lord? Do we even know how to do that?* Hezekiah challenged his priests and still challenges us not to be negligent and to make offerings to God. His priests answered his challenge. *Will we?*

Once the temple of the Lord had been restored to God, Hezekiah led the people in praise and worship. He saw that instruments were brought into the house of the Lord and songs of praise offered. The whole assembly "sang praises with gladness, and they bowed down and worshiped" (2 Chronicles 29:30b). Such worship and praise had not been offered in many years, but Hezekiah cared enough, was compassionate enough, and loved God enough to see that proper worship was restored. Just think how strong you would have to be to reintroduce instruments and songs of praise to an assembly that had ceased to worship God. Hezekiah was that strong.

Hezekiah restored the observance of the Passover, which had not been widely observed since the days of Solomon. This was especially important because it represented the bringing together of all of the tribes and served to reunify the divided kingdoms of Israel and Judah. After this observance, the people returned to their own towns and destroyed the idol altars and returned to the worship of God. The people also began to bring their tithes to the storehouse, and there was plenty for all because the Lord blessed them. Every work that Hezekiah "undertook in the service of the house of God, and in accordance with the law and the commandments, to seek his God, he did with all his heart; and he prospered" (2 Chronicles 31:21). He was strong in heart. *Do you think you could have reinstated the Passover observance and reunited the people? Could you have convinced the people to bring their tithes into the storehouse? Do you tithe and encourage others to tithe? Do you expect and receive a blessing?*

When King Sennacherib of Assyria invaded Judah and

sought to fight and capture her, Hezekiah told his people not to be afraid, because the one with them was greater than the one with their enemy. Sennacherib sent messengers to try to discourage Hezekiah's people by telling them that Hezekiah was misleading them and that they would all die. Sennacherib boasted about his many victories and that the God they served was no better than the gods of the many people he had defeated. But Hezekiah and the prophet Isaiah prayed to God. Sennacherib was defeated and returned to his land in disgrace and was subsequently murdered by his sons.

Although peace and prosperity came again to the land, Hezekiah became deathly ill. Isaiah told Hezekiah to set his house in order for he would not recover. Hezekiah prayed and cried to God for mercy and healing. God told Isaiah that he had heard Hezekiah's prayers and had seen his tears and would therefore add fifteen years to his life (Isaiah 38:5). Hezekiah was strong enough to cry and to accomplish great things throughout his reign. *Would you have begged and cried to God for length of days? Would you have used your additional days to continue your work for the Lord?* Hezekiah did.

Lord, hear my cries when I am in need, and strengthen me to work for you all the days of my life. Amen.

Manasseh

⌖

2 Chronicles 33:1-17

*U*nlike his father, Hezekiah, Manasseh was an evil king. He reigned for fifty-five years and did all he could to restore the abominable practices of the nations that the Lord drove out of Israel. He built altars to Baal, erected idols in the very house of the Lord in Jerusalem, practiced soothsaying and sorcery, and dealt with mediums and wizards. He does not sound like a very compassionate man, and for many years he wasn't. In fact, he "misled Judah and the inhabitants of Jerusalem, so that they did more evil than the nations whom the LORD had destroyed before the people of Israel" (2 Chronicles 33:9).

God spoke to Manasseh and his people and tried to get them to repent, but they would not listen. So God allowed the Assyrians to invade Judah. Manasseh was captured and taken in manacles and fetters to Babylon. While bound in prison, Manasseh sought the Lord. He reviewed all of his transgressions and repented of his numerous sins. He prayed that God would forgive him and restore him to his kingdom. He was strong, but he expressed great humility. His prayer is recorded in the Apocrypha, and he admits that his sins are greater in number than the sand of the sea. He claims that he is not worthy to look up and see the height of heaven and he claims that he is weighed down with sin. I can just feel the depth of his emotion as he says, "And now I bend the knee of my heart, imploring you for your kindness" (The Prayer of Manasseh, verse 11). *How does one bend the knee of one's heart?* One must lay one's heart bent and broken before God seeking true forgiveness and restoration. That is just what Manasseh did, and God forgave him. *Are you strong and brave enough to bend the knee of your heart before God? How earnestly do you seek forgiveness?*

When Manasseh was restored to his kingdom, he removed the idols and altars he had built to foreign gods, and future sacrifices were made only to the Lord. Like Asa, Manasseh cried and prayed to the Lord, and his prayer was answered: "Then Manasseh knew that the LORD indeed was God" (2 Chronicles 33:13*b*). Manasseh's heart was strong enough to bend before God and not break. He was a man who repented of his evil ways and became a compassionate man. *Can someone whom you consider to be "evil" because of the things he or she has done truly change? Is repentance primarily something we initiate, or is it God's grace that enables repentance?*

Dear God, I bend the knee of my heart in humble submission to you. Amen.

Nehemiah

*N*ehemiah lived comfortably in Susa. He held the high post of cupbearer, or wine taster, in the Persian court. He could have continued to live in this great position, but he had a compassionate heart. He asked his brother, Hanani, about the welfare of the Jews who had returned to Jerusalem from their Babylonian exile. When he heard the report of their trouble and the destruction of Jerusalem, he wept. Yes, he had a compassionate heart.

But weeping was not all that he did. He fasted, prayed, and started to execute a plan to improve the condition of the Jews whom he loved. As his position required, he took wine to King Artaxerxes, but his face was sad and his heart was heavy. The king noticed his distress and asked him what was wrong. Nehemiah explained the terrible condition of the home of his ancestors. The king asked how he might offer assistance, and Nehemiah requested permission to go to Judah to help rebuild it. He also asked for letters of recommendation to the governors of the area so that he might be granted safe passage, as well as a letter to the keeper of the king's forest requesting timber for the rebuilding. Nehemiah was in a position of power and was not afraid to ask for what he needed to rebuild the wall. He desperately wanted to help a troubled people, his own people, return to their God. *Have you ever been in a position like this to help others? Were you reluctant to ask for what you needed? Were you afraid that your request might not be granted?* Nehemiah acted without reservation.

Nehemiah carefully proceeded with the plan God had given him. He said to the people, "You see the trouble we are in, how Jerusalem lies in ruins with its gates burned. Come, let us rebuild the wall of Jerusalem, so that we may no longer suffer disgrace" (Nehemiah 2:17). He assured the people that the king was in full support and that God was in the plan and would give them success. The people agreed to help with the rebuilding. Although they were mocked and ridiculed for undertaking such an enormous project, Nehemiah insisted that God would enable them to achieve their goal. Nehemiah had a strong prayer life, and he allowed God to direct his life. He knew that the wall would be rebuilt. *How strong is your prayer life? Do you ever know with conviction that God will grant you success?*

Nehemiah cared enough to see that the disgruntled forces that opposed him were quieted and that the people were successful in the rebuilding. After the rebuilding was completed, Nehemiah returned to his position at court. But he kept in touch with Jerusalem and returned when he heard of the Jews' sinful decline. Nehemiah was not the type of man who, after giving aid, simply forgot about his people. He did not relax in the lap of luxury and pat himself on the back for having led the Jews in the rebuilding of the wall. He continuously joined forces with Ezra and was active in leading the Jews back to God. *What about you? Do you tend to relax after a major accomplishment, or do you continuously inquire to see that your successes prevail?* Nehemiah was the type who could answer that question positively. He was strong in heart.

Lord, remove my contented laziness, and motivate me to lead others to work for you. Amen.

Mordecai

ESTHER 2:5-11; 3:1-6; 4

M ordecai was kind and compassionate enough to assume the care of his orphaned cousin, Esther. He could have tried to find some other relative to care for her, but he cared enough to adopt her as his own daughter.

The book of Esther opens by setting the context of the story of Mordecai and Esther. In the third year of his reign, the Persian king Ahasuerus threw two huge banquets in the capital, one for the ministers and officials of the court and one for the people of Susa. Ahasuerus was interested in displaying the measure of his wealth and power to the political officials as well as to his subjects. However, the festivities took an unexpected turn when Ahasuerus called for the beautiful Queen Vashti to come to the banquet so that he could show her off. But she refused to be put on display. He was so enraged by her disobedience that he sent her away, decreeing that she should never enter his presence again.

On the advice of his servants, the king decreed that all of the beautiful young virgins in the kingdom be gathered so he could choose a replacement for Vashti. Wanting the best possible marriage for his adopted daughter, Mordecai took

Esther to the palace in response to the appeal for beautiful young virgins to replace Queen Vashti. *Do you think that today's parents should be more involved in making suitable marriages for their children? Do you think that Mordecai did the right thing?*

Mordecai's father had been among the Israelites taken from Jerusalem and taken captive to Babylon, where his family had continued to live. So when Esther was taken to the palace, Mordecai instructed her to conceal her Jewish lineage. Esther found favor with Hegai, the servant in charge of the women, so she and seven other women were chosen to be presented to the king. Esther and the others underwent a twelve-month beauty regime in preparation for their meeting with the king. "Every day Mordecai would walk around in front of the court of the harem, to learn how Esther was and how she fared" (Esther 2:11). After the long months of preparation, Esther was finally brought before the king and was chosen to be his queen. *How often do we leave our children in the care of others and never inquire how they are doing?* Mordecai cared, and he constantly inquired.

Mordecai found out about a plot to assassinate the king and told the newly crowned queen about it. He was able to prevent the assassination because when the plot was investigated, it was found to be so. Mordecai did not stand idly by and refuse to become involved when the king was threatened. He cared. *Would you have dared to get involved in a plot like this? Would you have thought that by telling Esther you were involving her and jeopardizing her place in the palace?* Mordecai was compassionate enough to take that chance.

Haman, an official in the court, was promoted by the king to the highest office in the land. Befitting his newly elevated status, the king also decreed that all members of the court were to bow down before him. However, Mordecai refused to do so. Mordecai knew that he could not bow down and do obeisance to Haman, for he realized that Haman was just a man and did not deserve to be worshiped. Haman was furious at Mordecai's disobedience. When Haman discovered that Mordecai was a Jew, he decided to take out his wrath not only on Mordecai, but also on all Jews in the land. Haman convinced the king that the Jews were not following his laws and asked for permission to destroy them, which the king granted.

Mordecai got word to Esther that all of their people were to be destroyed. Although Esther was reluctant to go before the king, as she had not been summoned, Mordecai prevailed upon her saying, "Do not think that in the king's palace you will escape any more than all the other Jews. For if you keep silence at such a time as this, relief and deliverance will rise for the Jews from another quarter, but you and your father's family will perish. Who knows? Perhaps you have come to royal dignity for just such a times as this" (Esther 4:13-14). *Would Mordecai's words have challenged you? Would you have responded the way Esther did?*

Mordecai was instrumental in convincing Esther to go to the king and save the Jews. He cared about his orphaned cousin, about his God, and about his people. He was a strong man of compassion.

God, give me the wisdom to recognize the specific purpose to which you have led me. Give me the strength to risk death to fulfill that purpose. Amen.

Job

JOB 1; 42

*I*f ever there was a man who was strong in heart, it had to have been Job. We always remember that he was long-suffering, but he was also strong and compassionate. Just think, he had a large family, houses, animals, and land. He knew and loved God and was righteous and upright in every way. It was probably easy for him to love God. He was blessed. *Isn't it easy for you to love God when everything is going well? But what happens when you suffer adversity?*

There are certain situations in life that everyone experiences. There is suffering, disappointment, and death at some point in everyone's life. Job not only experienced all of these, but also experienced them all at once. His blessed world was disrupted by the sudden death of his children and the loss of his possessions. Job responded to these losses by saying, "Naked I came from my mother's womb, and naked shall I return there; the LORD gave, and the LORD has taken away; blessed be the name of the LORD" (Job 1:21). His love for God did not allow him to blame God for his losses. *How do you deal with loss?*

Job was tested further when he lost his good health. *It is easy to praise God when one feels well, but what happens when health fails? Can you praise God when you are hurting?* Job could. His wife encouraged him to curse God and die, but Job told her how foolish she was being and said, "Shall we receive the good at the hand of God, and not receive the bad?" (Job 2:10*b*). *Have you ever pondered that question? Why is it that we only want the good that God has to offer?* Suffering is also a part of our lives. Job knew that.

Then Job's friends came around. They did not recognize him because of his poor condition and were convinced that he had surely sinned against God to be visited by such calamity. I wonder how many friends like this we have. *Do our friends assume that we have sinned when misfortune surrounds us? Do you ever make that assumption about your friends?* Job let his friends know—in no uncertain terms—that he had no sins to confess. He had remained faithful to God, and God was still in control of his life. Job declared that he would maintain his innocence, even before God. He said to them, "Though he slay me, yet will I trust in him: but I will maintain mine own ways before him" (Job 13:15 KJV). Job felt unjustly accused by his friends and, and, in fact, longed to plead his case before God. He was certain of his innocence and wanted to be vindicated. He boldly pronounced, "I know that my Redeemer lives, and that at last he will stand upon the earth; and after my skin has been thus destroyed, then in my flesh I shall see God, whom I shall see on my side, and my eyes shall behold, and not another" (Job 19:25-27).

As Job struggled to come to a deeper, more realistic knowledge and understanding of God, his bold pronouncement of actually seeing God came true. In a conversation with God he was successfully able to plead his case before God who spoke to him from a whirlwind. Job said to God, "I had heard of you by the hearing of the ear, but now my eye sees you" (Job 42:5). Job finally understood that he had been wrong to assert his innocence and demand an explanation from God. Suffering does happen, and it is not up to us to understand how it fits into God's plan. But Job was reassured that God, the creator, is still very much in control, and was reminded that he must trust in the goodness and power of God. *How do we see God? Have you ever had such a visionary experience? Were you frightened? Did you feel unworthy?* Job did, for he said, "Therefore I despise myself, and repent in dust and ashes" (Job 42:6). It is easy to get lost in the despair of our own painful situations. *Why is it important for us to gain a larger perspective at these times? In what ways are you reminded of God's loving presence and care in such situations?*

Job was called upon to show compassion for the friends who had pleaded with him to confess his sins. God sent those same friends to him for prayer and sacrifice. Job offered prayer for them, for he knew that they had not seen God as he had. *Could you forgive the friends who had insisted that you had sinned when you knew that you had not? Could you pray for them?* Job did.

God restored Job's blessings twofold. His latter days were more blessed than his former ones. His daughters were the most beautiful women in the land, and he lived to see four generations of his family. Yes, Job was strong in his faith and his convictions. But he was also a man of compassion—a quality no doubt deepened by his own sufferings.

Lord, keep me unattached to earthly treasures, for I brought nothing into this world, and I can take nothing with me. Help me always to trust that you are in control, even when things in my life and in the world don't seem to be. Amen.

Isaiah

❦

*O*ften called the greatest of the Old Testament prophets, Isaiah served the Lord during a turbulent time. The kingdom of Judah was dallying with foreign powers and trying to make political alliances. There were deals involving the quest for power and luxury. When God needed someone to speak to the people about their sin and disobedience, Isaiah volunteered. I wonder about the depth and strength of compassion it must have taken to volunteer for such a job!

In the year that King Uzziah died, Isaiah saw a vision of God sitting on a throne. Because evil deeds were rampant, perhaps Isaiah could not see all that surrounded him. Isaiah seems to have been fascinated with King Uzziah because he did not or could not see the Lord. But when King Uzziah died, Isaiah saw the Lord. The fact that he saw the Lord high and lifted up has some significance. If his vision of the Lord had been in some low place, he might have overlooked him. But the Lord was high and in a holy place. No doubt Isaiah feared for his life. In the presence of the holy Lord of hosts, Isaiah also recognized and confessed his own unworthiness to stand before God: "And [he] said, 'Woe is me! I am lost, for I am a man of unclean lips, and I live among a people of unclean lips; yet my eyes have seen the King, the LORD of hosts!'" (Isaiah 6:5). I wonder how many of us recognize our own unworthiness before the Lord. *Do you?*

Isaiah expressed real sorrow that he was lost and did not speak or live to the glory of God. He also regretted that the people around him were guilty of the same transgressions. Realizing his sin, he expressed amazement that he actually had seen the real king, not Uzziah, but the Lord of hosts! Then one of the seraphs took a hot coal from the altar and held it to Isaiah's mouth and purified him of his sins.

Isaiah's vision gives us all hope. Even though we live unworthy lives and live among others who do the same, there is still the possibility that we will see God. Once we see him, we, like Isaiah, must respond to God's call. Without hesitation, Isaiah volunteered, though he had no idea what task he had signed on for. Isaiah had the awesome task of informing the people that they would be chastised and that only a remnant of them would survive. This remnant would continue to do the work of the Lord.

Can you imagine the strength it must have taken to deliver news of divine judgment to the people? Can you imagine how Isaiah's message was received? Who would believe this man who had sinned just as the people had? Who would believe one whose fascination with the king was apparent? Surely the people must have thought him crazy and arrogant. *After all, who was he to speak on the behalf of God?* Even knowing what the response to him would be, Isaiah accepted God's call to be a prophet to the people. He was a great prophet. He sought to convince the people to respond to the God who was the real king. His message, like that of so many prophets before and after him, was not heeded. He expressed his frustration in the names of his sons, Shear-jashub (a remnant will return) and Mahershalalhashbaz (the spoil speeds, the prey hastens) (Henry H. Halley, *Bible Handbook* [Chicago: Henry H. Halley, 1959]).

His vision was clear; his prophetic voice would be heard even if unheeded.

It takes strength to stand and speak before a people living in sin. One might not even agree to do this if one were drafted. But Isaiah volunteered. He was strong in heart and had compassion for the people. *What about you?*

Lord, I want to volunteer for your service. Keep my vision clear and focused on you, and let my voice be heard. Amen.

Jeremiah

❧

JEREMIAH 1

*E*ven though he resisted his prophetic calling because he was only a boy, Jeremiah became a strong man and was so filled with compassion that he was known as the weeping prophet.

Just how did Jeremiah become known as the weeping prophet? We know that he descended from the priests of Anathoth, a village northeast of Jerusalem. We know that God knew him and his destiny before he was born and that he was called as a youth. We know that Judah was in great decline, for its inhabitants failed to walk in the ways of the Lord. We know that Jeremiah was called to prophesy to people who made offerings to other gods and worshiped idols. We know that Jeremiah was told that the people would resist him and would rise up against him, but he was assured that God would be with him and would not forsake him. Perhaps this was reason enough to weep.

But Jeremiah wept not because of the enormous task that was before him. He wept because the people would not listen and continued to live in wickedness. He wept because he had to oppose his king. He wept because he was arrested. He wept because he was fought and threatened throughout his career. He wept because he loved God and hated the people's continuing disobedience. *Haven't you felt like weeping when your loved ones ignore your counsel and continue on destructive paths?* I know that I have, and Jeremiah did.

Even though his prophecy was ignored, Jeremiah continued to proclaim his message. He felt compelled to preach. He even said, "If I say 'I will not mention him [God], or speak any more in his name,' then within me there is something like a burning fire shut up in my bones. I am weary with holding it in, and I cannot" (Jeremiah 20:9). *Have you ever felt that type of fire burning within that compelled you to speak?* If you have, then you know that Jeremiah had reason to weep.

Jeremiah dared to tell King Zedekiah that there was a word from the Lord. Jeremiah reported that Jerusalem would be captured and burned by the Babylonians. He therefore urged the king to surrender to the Babylonian king so that Jerusalem might not be destroyed. But the king did not want to hear such news, and Jeremiah's prophecy was labeled as treason. He was captured and left to die in an abandoned cistern. Ebed-melech, an Ethiopian in the king's court, persuaded Zedekiah to allow him to rescue Jeremiah from the cistern in which Jeremiah would surely starve to death. Jeremiah was eventually taken to Egypt. He had warned his nation not to enter into alliances with Egypt, but of course he was ignored.

When God's judgment on the people was carried out through the Babylonian army, Jeremiah wept as Jerusalem fell to the enemy; yet he remembered God's love and faithfulness to the people and knew that God longed for their return.

Would you have been strong enough to preach when no one wanted to hear? Would you have wept over the sins of your people? Would you have dared to tell your king that there was a word from the Lord? How would you have handled being the only one speaking for God?

Jeremiah was a man of great compassion. He remained

strong enough to prophesy his whole life long. He was not distracted from his calling—no matter how great his distress. He just wept and continued to call Judah to repentance. I wonder whether there is a Jeremiah for this present age. *Do we need a weeping prophet? Would we listen to him or her?*

Lord, sometimes I feel like weeping because of the sins of the world, but I know that you need me to do more than weep. Equip me to do your will. Amen.

Ebed-melech

❧

JEREMIAH 38:7-12; 39:16-18

*E*bed-melech was an Ethiopian serving in the court of King Zedekiah just before Judah was occupied by Babylon. He was a man of great compassion who rescued Jeremiah from the underground cistern in which he had been imprisoned for treason. He could have pretended that he did not know Jeremiah was in the cistern. He could have failed to ask the king if he could rescue Jeremiah. He could have concentrated on his own life and the troubles that were coming to Judah. But he didn't. He took the time to care and to become involved.

Ebed-melech told the king about the wicked deed that had been done to Jeremiah. He knew that, left unattended, Jeremiah would surely die and asked for permission to rescue Jeremiah. The king not only gave his permission, but also ordered Ebed-melech to take three men with him to help rescue Jeremiah. Having been granted permission to attempt the rescue, Ebed-melech went to a wardrobe of the king's house and got some old clothes and rags and let those down to Jeremiah by ropes. He took the time and was concerned enough to tell Jeremiah to put the rags and clothes between his armpits and the ropes so he and the men could pull him to safety without pain. Ebed-melech was both strong and compassionate and he dared to save Jeremiah from certain death.

King Zedekiah had the opportunity to listen to the vision and prophecy of the rescued Jeremiah, but he still did not take heed. Jeremiah advised Zedekiah to surrender to the king of Babylon so that his life and the lives of those in his household would be spared. Zedekiah ignored this advice and was later captured when Jerusalem fell to the Babylonian army. His sons were murdered before his very eyes, and then his eyes were put out after witnessing the tragedy. His houses were burned, and he was bound and taken to Babylon.

Jeremiah was also taken to Babylon and held, though King Nebuchadnezzar of Babylon made certain that Jeremiah was not harmed, perhaps because he knew that Jeremiah had advised Zedekiah to surrender. Ebed-melech's good deed to Jeremiah eventually saved his own life. God instructed Jeremiah to send word to Ebed-melech that he would also be spared when the city was destroyed because of his trust in God. It is a good thing that he was a strong man of compassion who had chosen to get involved.

Are you brave enough to get involved, or do you just ignore the troubles that surround you? Would you have been compassionate enough to think to use clothes between the ropes and Jeremiah's armpits so that he would not feel pain while being rescued from the pit? Ebed-melech is a good example of a biblical man of compassion.

Lord, make me brave enough to get involved in the injustices that surround me. There may be a Jeremiah I can help rescue. Amen.

Shadrach, Meshach, and Abednego

DANIEL 3

*D*aniel, Shadrach, Meshach, and Abednego were young Hebrew noblemen serving in the court of the Babylonian king, Nebuchadnezzar. After the capture of Jerusalem, Nebuchadnezzar ordered that bright young members of the Hebrew court be chosen and brought to Babylon for training to serve in the Babylonian court. Daniel and his three friends were among the young men chosen, and they were taken to Babylon where they received training in the language and literature of Babylon.

Daniel and his friends were handsome, strong, and bright; and they excelled in their training, finding favor both with their teachers and with the king. They ate only vegetables and drank only water and refused the royal rations of King Nebuchadnezzar, but God saw to it that they prospered and were extremely healthy. "To these four young men God gave knowledge and skill in every aspect of literature and wisdom; Daniel also had insight into all visions and dreams" (Daniel 1:17). These young Hebrews became trusted advisors to the king who found their wisdom and counsel ten times better than that of all of the "magicians and enchanters" in the kingdom. After Daniel interpreted

Nebuchadnezzar's troubling dream (after all of the wise men of Babylon had been unable to do so), the king rewarded him by making Daniel ruler over the whole province of Babylon. At Daniel's request, Shadrach, Meshach, and Abednego were also promoted to rule over the affairs of the province.

Everything went well until the king had a golden statue made, and all of the officials of the provinces were assembled for its dedication. At the dedication, the herald announced that at the sound of the musical ensemble everyone was to bow down and worship the golden statue, and all who failed to do so would be thrown into a fiery furnace. Shadrach, Meshach, and Abednego, however, refused to bow down to the statue. A group of Chaldean officials in attendance—no doubt jealous of the high positions that had been given to Jews—informed the king that the Hebrews refused to bow to the statue and to worship the Babylonian gods. Of course, their disobedience and insubordination was a great insult to the king, and he was furious. He sent for the three and gave them one last chance to worship his gods and the golden statue. He warned them that if they did not comply with the order, they would be thrown into a blazing furnace. *What would you have done?*

In a tone of compassion, Shadrach, Meshach, and Abednego told the king that they meant no disrespect and had no need to present a defense. They believed that the God they served was able to deliver them from the furnace, but that if not, they still would not serve the king's gods or bow down to his statue. The king was so offended by their words that his face was distorted, and he ordered that they be thrown into the furnace that was to be made seven times hotter than normal.

The Hebrew boys were bound and thrown into the furnace. The fire was so hot that it killed the men who threw them in. But Shadrach, Meshach, and Abednego appeared to be unharmed. When King Nebuchadnezzar looked into the furnace, he was startled to see four men, the fourth having the appearance of a god. All were walking around, unbound and unharmed. The king could not believe his eyes. He approached the furnace and called to the Hebrew boys and told them to come out. When they did, everyone present saw that they were unharmed—their hair was not singed, their clothes were not damaged, and there was no smell of smoke about them.

The Apocrypha records the prayer of praise that was recited by the Hebrews while they were in the furnace. They claimed complete devotion to God and asked for mercy and deliverance. This portion of the Apocrypha is included in the Additions to Daniel and is entitled "The Prayer of Azariah [the Hebrew name for Abednego] and the Song of the Three Jews." The prayer recalls the deliverance of the Jews in difficult situations and expresses the belief that the same God would deliver them. *Do you pray prayers of praise and adoration in difficult situations? Do you have confidence that you will be delivered?*

King Nebuchadnezzar decreed that no one should speak against the God of Shadrach, Meshach, and Abednego, for their God had delivered them in a way no other god could. These Hebrew boys were strong, fearless, and willing to sacrifice their lives for the God who could and would save them. Although often referred to as boys, they were men of great compassion.

Lord, I am grateful that I do not have to face a fiery furnace, but sometimes the trials I do face seem awfully hot. Be with me as you were with the Hebrew boys, and I will give you the glory and the praise. Amen.

Daniel

❦

When it comes to compassion, Daniel cannot in any way be excluded. We know he was strong and courageous, as were his companions, Shadrach, Meshach, and Abednego. We know that he faithfully served King Nebuchadnezzar, the Babylonian king, though he was living as an exiled captive after the fall of Jerusalem. He gave the king wise counsel and interpreted the meaning of a troubling dream, though one might imagine that Daniel was not pre-disposed to provide such loyal service to his captor. But Daniel did not deny his God-given gifts and did what the king asked. As a result of his interpretative powers, he was made ruler over the province of Babylon

Daniel continued to serve in the court under Nebuchadnezzar's son, King Belshazzar, who is described in somewhat unflattering terms. Belshazzar threw a huge party for his lords and court officials as an extravagant display of his wealth and power. After drinking to excess, Belshazzar and his guests decided to use the gold and silver vessels taken from the temple in Jerusalem and brought to Babylon by his father. Whenever the Babylonians were successful in battle, it was their practice to take the religious statues of their captive's gods or icons from their holy places. In the case of the Jews, the ritual vessels were taken since there were no idols or statues in the Temple in Jerusalem. The symbolic significance of taking these religious items to Babylon was to show the subordinate status of the conquered people and their gods. Belshazzar's use of them as mere drinking vessels was a denigration of these holy objects dedicated to the worship of God. Even worse, we are told that Belshazzar and his guests not only drank from these vessels, but also "praised the gods of silver and gold, of bronze, iron, wood, and stone" as they drank (Daniel 5:23).

Immediately after this act of idolatry, Belshazzar had a frightening vision of a human hand writing on the wall of the palace. Obviously shaken by this terrifying vision, Belshazzar sent for all of the wise men in his territory, but no one was able to interpret the handwriting on the wall. Noticing that the wise men were unsuccessful, Belshazzar's mother, the queen, told him about Daniel's God-given gifts that enabled him to interpret. She told him of the position Daniel had held under King Nebuchadnezzar and how much wisdom and knowledge he had. She was convinced that Daniel would be able to help King Belshazzar.

Daniel was sent for, and the king told him of the gifts and high position—including making him the third-highest ranking official in the kingdom—that would be his if he could and would interpret the handwriting. Daniel rejected the gifts and did not need or want the position of third in the kingdom. He cared enough simply to share the gift that God had given him. He informed Belshazzar that his father had been stripped of his kingdom because of his pride and arrogance, believing that he held absolute power and control over the lives of his subjects. Because of this position, his father, Nebuchadnezzar, was driven away from human society and dwelt in the wilderness living like an animal for a time (see Daniel 4). Daniel warned Belshazzar that he was traveling down the same path. Even though he was aware of what had happened to his father, Belshazzar continued to drink wine and worship idol gods rather than honor the true God who had given him life and breath. Daniel broke the news that God had numbered the days of his kingdom and had brought it to an end. The kingdom would be divided and given to the Medes and Persians (Daniel 5:26-27). That very night, events happened just as Daniel predicted. Belshazzar was killed, and Darius, the Mede, was given the kingdom. *Would you have been strong enough to deliver this interpretation to the king? Would you have feared for your life?*

Under the reign of Darius, Daniel was appointed one of the three "presidents," or "satraps," that ruled over all of the regions and continued to prosper. His wisdom was greater than that of all others, and the other presidents and satraps tried to find a complaint to bring against him. Finding none, they came up with a plan to cast into a den of lions anyone who prayed to anyone other than King Darius for a period of thirty days. They knew that Daniel prayed three times a day to his God, and the only way they could find a complaint against him would have to be in connection with his observance of the law of his God. *If someone were trying to bring a complaint against you, would it be safe to assume that it would be in connection with your worship of God? Or would they have to find something or someone to whom you are more devoted?*

But Daniel was faithful and fearless. Knowing that the document forbidding his prayers had been signed, he went home, knelt before the open window, and prayed to his God. The jealous satraps reminded the king of his edict and informed him of Daniel's disobedience to the decree. Reluctant to punish Daniel, the king made every effort to save him but could not. (Once a decree was signed by the king, it became law and could not be revoked—even by the king.) Daniel had to be thrown into the den of lions. The king said to Daniel, "May your God, whom you faithfully serve, deliver you!" (Daniel 6:16b). After Daniel was taken, the king went to the palace and fasted. *If you were taken to an almost certain death, would anyone fast and pray for you? Would you have had the courage to defy the law so openly?*

The next morning the king rushed to the den to find Daniel alive and well. Daniel reported that God had sent angels to close the mouths of the lions that would have devoured him. Daniel was indeed faithful and fearless.

Perhaps one of Daniel's strongest acts of compassion is recorded in Additions to Daniel in the Apocrypha. It is the story of Susanna, a young wife, who was wrongfully accused of adultery by two wicked judges who desired her. The judges tried to force Susanna to lie with them by threatening to report that she had committed adultery with another man. But she refused and declared that she would rather die for a sin that she did not commit than live with a sin that she had committed. True to their word, the spurned judges accused her of adultery, and she was sentenced to death.

It was Daniel who found a way to save Susanna. He did not stand by and allow a religious young woman to be wrongfully accused. He decided to do something about it. He devised a plan to catch the judges in their lies, and Susanna's life was spared. *How many times do we stand idly by and allow the innocent to be accused and convicted?* Daniel did not, for he was indeed a strong and compassionate man.

Lord, if you need me to face the lions of this world, be with me. If you need me to be a detective to save your children, equip me. If you need me to set an example as a prayer warrior, give me wise words and strong knees. Amen.

Hosea

⤿

HOSEA 1; 3

*W*hat a compassionate and loving man Hosea must have been to agree to take a promiscuous wife and have children of promiscuity. Why would God ask Hosea to do this? Perhaps the second half of God's instructions to Hosea gives us a clue: "for the land commits great whoredom by forsaking the LORD" (Hosea 1:2*b*). Hosea loved a woman, the prostitute Gomer, who could not promise to love him back exclusively. Hosea could not be sure that any children born of the union were his. Their very names, Jezreel, meaning "God sows," Loruhamah, meaning "no more pity," and Loammi, meaning "not my people," reflected Hosea's feeling about their parentage.

But we know that Hosea acted symbolically for God. Israel was aware that God had provided for Israel. God had brought the people out of bondage in Egypt and guided and sustained them as they crossed the wilderness to the promised land. But Israel had deserted God and had gone whoring after other gods. As a result of their disobedience and unfaithfulness, God told them they would reap what they had sown. They would no longer be pitied and were no longer to be counted among the people of God.

Yet, even though Israel had deserted God, God did not desert Israel. God used the compassionate Hosea to demonstrate his unfailing love. *Could God have used you in this way?* Time and again Hosea took back his wayward wife just as God had repeatedly taken back Israel. The strong and compassionate Hosea was sensitive to the acts and practices of the society in which he lived. Time and again he had indicted Israel for deserting God, and yet he could still describe the love, patience, and forgiveness of God.

The Israelites would sometimes cling to their idols and cry out to God. Hosea tenderly described God's loving care for Israel even though they sought idols. He reminded the people how they had been taught to walk and had been kissed and fed. Though Israel was bent on turning away, God could not give them up. God did not respond to them as a human being would; God responded to them as only God could— with forgiveness. *How would you have responded to them?*

Hosea's treatment of his unfaithful wife set the example of unlimited love, grace, and mercy that God demonstrated for the unfaithful people of Israel. Just listening to his prophecy had to remind Israel of the great compassion of God. Hosea was indeed a man of strength and love.

Lord, I don't know if I could have done what Hosea did, but I do understand your unconditional love for me. Help me love and serve you faithfully. I know that I cannot reciprocate your love, but I will give it all I've got. Amen.

Amos

༄

*A*mos was not from a long line of prophets or from the aristocracy. He was a poor shepherd from Tekoa, a village south of Bethlehem in Judea. Why was a shepherd chosen to preach to a people who had immoral practices, relied on military prowess, dealt unjustly with society, and worshiped idols? Perhaps it was because Amos, as his name implies, was a "burden bearer." He understood what was happening to the people of Israel and cared enough to bear the burden of communicating what God revealed to him.

Amos was a simple, untrained man, but he understood what sin was. He knew that power should not be misused and that wealth should not be acquired unjustly. He understood what it meant to care about people and wanted Israel to feel compassion for those who were suffering. Amos had a compassionate heart and was not afraid to risk rejection. *Have you ever cared enough to risk communicating an unpopular message to someone who you knew was sinning?*

Amos tried to ease Israel into repentance. He began his prophecy by explaining the sins of neighboring people. He talked about those who had disobeyed in Damascus, Gaza, Tyre, Edom, and Ammon. He reiterated the sins of Moab and Judah and then lowered the boom. Perhaps he believed that if Israel first saw the sins of others, they might be more willing to see their own sins. *Isn't it human nature to want to see the sins of others and feel just a little proud that we are not like them?* Amos was actually setting the people of Israel up for their own message of sinful behavior.

The message Amos delivered was strong and powerful. He told of cheating the righteous and the needy, of the sexual sins of a father and son with the same woman, and of defaming the altar of God. He told them how God had brought them out of bondage in Egypt and had raised up prophets among them. In spite of all God had done for the Israelites, they were unfaithful and had turned away from God. Amos urged the Israelites to repent—to seek God and live and to "let justice roll down like waters, and righteousness like an ever-flowing stream" (Amos 5:24).

Amos used imagery that was simple and familiar. He wanted Israel to understand God's judgment if they did not repent. He used a basket of fruit that was beautiful on the outside but rotten on the inside. He used a plumb line that could measure accurately the crooked and corrupt places that needed to be torn down and rebuilt. Amos cared enough to make it plain.

The priest of Bethel, Amaziah, accused Amos of treason for his prophecies of destruction and exile of the Israelites and asked him to leave Israel. Amos left, but his message lived on. He did what the Lord told him to do. He tried to redeem the Israelites because he cared about them. He was strong and brave. For Amos to deliver such an unwelcome message of judgment surely took great strength and courage. He was a biblical man of compassion.

Lord, I need a plumb line so that I can accurately measure my life. Be my plumb line, and keep me grounded and rooted in your Word. Amen.

Habakkuk

*H*abakkuk was distressed by all of the violence and sin around him. Even worse, he was grieved by the fact that God didn't seem to be listening, though he continued to pray that God would set things right. He wondered how long he would have to cry for help. He wondered why he was permitted to see the violence and sin that surrounded him. He wondered what he could do to bring about change. The righteous suffered under the oppression of the wicked. Habakkuk was compassionately concerned about his nation and longed for justice and righteousness.

Out of his concern, Habakkuk decided to stand at the watchpost and wait for a word from the Lord. But God surprised Habakkuk when God told him to write down the vision. God told him to make it plain on tablets so that runners passing by could read it. God told Habakkuk that there was still a vision for the appointed time and that vision did not lie. Habakkuk was instructed to wait for it, for it would surely come. God assured Habbakkuk that the vision he was being given was trustworthy and would come to pass and that justice would be restored. *Do you sometimes wonder why evil exists but God doesn't fix it?*

What would you have done in Habakkuk's place? Would you have complained and decided to wait for a word from the Lord? How would you have responded to the dominance of people of other nations, more wicked than your own? Would you have assumed the responsibility of writing the vision for a wicked and perverse people? Would you have posted it on tablets so that runners could see it? Would you have been willing to wait for your vision to become a reality? Habakkuk was compassionate and strong, so he was willing to do what God instructed.

Habakkuk wrote the vision. He prophesied death and destruction to the people of Judah. Their pride, greed, and wickedness would be their undoing. Their glory would turn to shame, and the idols they worshiped would be revealed as worthless. He told them that the Lord was in his holy temple and that he would rejoice in the Lord who was his strength and his salvation.

Habakkuk may have felt like a lone voice crying in the wilderness of violence and sin; yet, he cried on. He wrote the vision. He expressed his concern. He was a man of strength and compassion.

God, let me live in such a way that others know that I have a vision that is so plain that runners can read it in my life as they pass by. Help me remember that in spite of all of the evil and sadness in the world, you are still in control and have redeemed the world. Give me the strength and courage to help bring in your kingdom by fighting against injustice and oppression. Amen.

Tobit

TOBIT

In the Apocryphal book bearing his name, Tobit is described as one who walked in the ways of truth and righteousness all the days of his life and performed many acts of charity (Tobit 1:3). This description is certainly indicative of a man of compassion. He was a righteous and observant Jew, though he had been living in exile in Nineveh, the land of the Assyrians. His very name is translated "God is my good."

When Tobit traveled to the temple in Jerusalem, he offered not one or two tithes, but three. He knew that the money was needed for the widows and orphans and those who had converted to Judaism. Although he lived in Nineveh, he continued to observe the Jewish laws. He faithfully observed Jewish laws such as refusing to eat the Gentile food, feeding the hungry, clothing the naked, and burying the dead. God had rewarded him for his faithfulness, for he held a position in King Shalmaneser's court.

After the king died, his son Sennacherib assumed the throne and began executing many Jews. Tobit defied Sennacherib's edict that those executed by the state were not to be buried and secretly buried as many of the dead as he could. When Tobit's defiance was discovered, the king seized Tobit's property, and Tobit fled for his life. But before Tobit could be caught, Sennacherib was murdered by his son who assumed the throne. Tobit was able to return and resume his position in the court.

Later, Tobit received word that another Jew had been murdered and his body left in the marketplace without the benefit of proper burial. Of course, Tobit felt compelled to respond and hid the body until after sundown when he could bury it in secret. His neighbors did not understand why Tobit would continue to bury the dead when doing so had almost cost him his life in the past. But Tobit's righteousness and compassion made it impossible for him not to follow God's law. After he buried the man, Tobit went out to sleep in the coolness of the courtyard where sparrows' droppings fell in his eyes, causing him to become completely blind.

Tobit believed in God's righteousness but did not understand how he could continue to serve God in his blinded state. So he prayed for death. Believing that he would die, Tobit recalled that he had left some money with a relative in Media and asked his son Tobiah to get it so that there would be sufficient funds for his burial and the support of the family. He went about setting his affairs straight, making his son promise to care for his mother and encouraging him to find a wife among his people. He also advised Tobiah to worship and serve God all of his life, to be generous and not begrudging in giving, to drink only in moderation, and to share his food and clothing with others (Tobit 4:1-11). *What type of advice would you give to a son if you believed that you would soon die?*

Tobit showed additional concern and compassion for his son as he searched for a trustworthy person to accompany him on his journey to get the money that was left with the relative. He looked for someone who knew the way and would act as a guide and companion for his son. Although Tobit does not know it at the time, the man he found was an angel. He interviewed the man; he asked about his ancestry and whether the man knew the way. *I wonder how many of us send our children out with people we don't really know. Do you ever ask about the family of a potential companion for your children? Do you find out if they know the way to their destination?* Tobit did. He cared about his son.

On the journey to Media, Tobiah and his companion found a cure for Tobit's blindness and met Sarah, the daughter of the relative with whom they were staying. Sarah was a young widow who had been married seven times, only to have all of her husbands die before the marriage could be consummated. Tobiah's angelic companion suggested that he marry Sarah, thus performing the duty of a kinsman to care for a widowed relative. (Tobit had advised him to marry a relative.) Successfully married, they retrieve the money they were sent for, and after the wedding celebration, they return to Tobit. His sight was restored, and he welcomed his new daughter. Tobit lived to the age of 112 and praised God, saying, "Though he afflicted me, he has had mercy upon me" (Tobit 11:15a).

Tobit's life of compassion and acts of charity identify him as strong in heart. He went above and beyond the requirements of the Jewish law. *Have you ever considered giving a third tithe? Have you ever contributed to the cost of burial for one who died without insurance? What type of advice do you offer your children when they leave home on a journey? Do you have faith that they will carry out your wishes in the manner that you have requested?* Tobit had faith in God and in his son. He was a strong and compassionate man.

Lord, I want to be a wise parent and faithful servant who gives more than is required, even beyond the tithe. Tobit set a good example. Amen.

Joseph

❧

MATTHEW 1:18-25

*J*ust imagine having to wait until the yearlong period of engagement was completed before you and your intended could become man and wife. At the end of that year you could finally consummate your relationship. But imagine that before that happened, your fiancée came to you with the news that she was pregnant. You knew that it could not be your child and were hurt that she had been unfaithful. *What would you do in a situation like this?*

Joseph decided to do what many men would. He was going to put Mary away quietly. He no longer wanted to marry her and did not want to raise a child who was not his. The punishment for adultery could be severe and humiliating, but Joseph was not willing to disgrace her publicly. His desire to send her away quietly gives us a glimpse of his compassionate spirit. What he felt compelled to do he intended to do quietly. But before he could act, God sent an angel in a dream to assure him that Mary had not been unfaithful.

We know the story. The angel told Joseph not to be afraid to take Mary as his wife, for the child she had conceived was not of man, but of the Holy Spirit. The child, who should be called Jesus, would save the people from their sins and would fulfill the prophecy from Isaiah concerning the Messiah: "'Look, the virgin shall conceive and bear a son, and they shall name him Emmanuel,' which means, 'God is with us'" (Matthew 1:23).

Don't you think that Joseph could have responded, "Yea, right! A child conceived by the Holy Spirit. Do you think I am a fool?" Men less righteous and faithful or men less compassionate probably would have responded in that way. But Joseph did not. He did what the angel of God commanded and married the pregnant Mary. Though married, he refrained from having relations with her until after the birth of the child.

Joseph assumed the full role of earthly father and protector. He took Mary and the child to Egypt to escape Herod and his intention to kill the child. He was later notified in a dream to take the child to the district of Galilee where he and Mary raised him. Joseph taught Jesus the ways of the Jewish faith and took him to Jerusalem at Passover. He taught him his trade of carpentry and in every way recognized and accepted Jesus as his own child.

What a testimony to compassion and strength! Joseph loved Mary and he loved the Lord. He was a wonderful earthly father for our Lord! *What kind of father would you have been?*

Lord, make me a good and willing parent to children who are not biologically mine. Amen.

The Wise Men

MATTHEW 2:1-12

*A*fter the birth of Jesus in Bethlehem, three travelers from the East arrived in Jerusalem, asking for information about the child who had been born the king of the Jews so they could pay homage to the child. Although they are often called kings and even given names in some traditions, the Gospel of Matthew simply identifies them as wise men. They were indeed wise, for they knew that a king had been born in Bethlehem and had recognized his unique star.

When King Herod, ruler of Judea, heard about the travelers and the baby for whom they were looking, he became frightened and called together the chief priests and scribes to find out more about the prophecies concerning the birth of the Messiah. Herod was understandably upset because this "king of the Jews" was a threat to his own power. Receiving a report of the time that the star had appeared and learning that the prophets had predicted the birth of the Messiah in Bethlehem, Herod sent for the wise men and asked them to tell him what they knew about the baby. He urged them to search diligently in Bethlehem for the child and report to him upon finding the child so that he might worship him also.

The wise men set out for Bethlehem and were guided by

the star that they had first seen rising in the East. When the star stopped over the place where the child lay, they were filled with joy. *Can you imagine the joy you might feel in knowing that you were about to see the Messiah?* Just think of the joy you feel when you first see your child or your new family member. It is an unspeakable joy.

The wise men did not approach the child empty-handed. They brought gifts of gold, frankincense, and myrrh. They loved this child and bowed down as they presented their gifts. Just think about the appropriateness of the gifts. The gold was a gift fit for a king, but this king would reign from a cross, not from a throne. The frankincense was a fragrant resin used for temple worship and sacrifice and was a gift fit for a priest. This child would teach us the meaning of true worship and would show us ultimate sacrifice. And myrrh was a fragrant resin used for anointing and for embalming, and was a gift fit for a king who would soon die. This body would not need to be embalmed, for it would rise from the dead. Although this last gift symbolized death, its preservation quality would be totally enhanced with a new embalming agent. That agent was eternal life. *Which of these gifts do you feel was the most appropriate? What would you have given?*

After worshiping the child, the wise men returned home without going back through Jerusalem and reporting to Herod. They had been warned in a dream to avoid Herod for the protection of the child. Not only was their disobedience an act of compassion, but also it was an act of strength and courage, for they risked Herod's wrath. Men who are strong in heart may have to risk disobedience to local authorities when the Holy Spirit guides them. *Has the Spirit ever led you to disobey local authorities? How did you respond? Were you as strong and compassionate as the wise men were?*

Lord, I want to give a special gift to Jesus. I know that the most fitting gift would be my heart. Help me give it completely. Amen.

The Centurion

MATTHEW 8:5-13

The Centurion, by his own admission, was a man in a position of power. As an officer of the Roman army, all he had to do was give a command and it would be obeyed. But the Centurion was also a man of compassion. He went looking for Jesus, not because he or his family needed healing, but because his servant did. *Have you ever sought help for a servant or hired hand?* Amazingly, the Centurion, a Gentile, addressed Jesus as Lord and appealed to him to cure his paralyzed servant. Without hesitation Jesus agreed to follow the Centurion home and heal his servant.

This is where the story gets interesting. The Centurion did not ask Jesus to follow him home. He did not even want Jesus to take the time to enter his home. He did not feel worthy of having Jesus in his home. *Would you have felt worthy enough to have Jesus in your home?* The Centurion knew that with the power and authority that Jesus had, it was not necessary for Jesus to be in the same place as his servant in order to heal him. All Jesus needed to do was speak the word and the servant would be healed.

The Centurion knew that he did not have the power that Jesus had. He knew that he could not heal his servant, but he knew that even in his position all he had to do was speak and those under his authority obeyed. If his feeble commands could be obeyed by his words, surely the words of the Lord could and would be obeyed. The Centurion had such faith that Jesus admitted that he had not seen anything like it in all of Israel. Because of this great faith, the servant was healed from a distance.

The Centurion felt compassion for his servant. He took the time to look for Jesus, who had been performing miracles of healing. He believed in the work and power of the Lord who had come in the name of the God of Israel. He was strong enough to risk being rejected, for surely he had heard that this Jesus had come only to the household of Israel. But he cared enough for his servant and he believed more than enough in the power of Jesus. *Would you have ventured out in search of Jesus for a servant of yours? Would you have risked rejection? Would you have believed in the healing power of one who was not of your religion?*

This strong man of compassion taught us all that if we have faith, the word spoken with power is sufficient for any need. *Have you ever asked Jesus to just speak the word?* The compassionate centurion did.

God, give me the bold faith of the Centurion. I want to believe that when you speak the word, it will be done. Help my unbelief. Amen.

Peter

MARK 1:30-31; ACTS 3:1-10

*A*lthough there are many stories in the New Testament that illustrate the strengths and weaknesses of Peter, I have chosen to concentrate on two brief stories, which I believe give a glimpse of Peter's compassion. The first one involves Peter's mother-in-law. From the text we can surmise that Peter's mother-in-law lived with him, his brother, Andrew, and his other family members. Having a live-in mother-in-law might in and of itself demonstrate Peter's compassion and strength. We might also assume that when Peter decided to take Jesus to his house, he knew that his mother-in-law was in bed with a fever.

Although the text does not specifically say that Peter asked Jesus to heal his mother-in-law, we are informed "they told him [Jesus] about her at once" (Mark 1:30*b*). Could the "they" in this case include Peter? I think it does because Peter seems to have a compassionate nature. The text continues with the statement that after being healed, Peter's mother-in-law got up and served them. Perhaps Peter felt some compassion for Jesus and his companions and knew that his mother-in-law was the best person to serve and satisfy their needs. I am sure that Peter wanted the best for those who had accompanied him to his house. His mother-in-law was probably the best cook in the house. *Have you ever invited guests to your house when the person who was to prepare the meal was ill? Have you wished that your guests had the power of healing?*

Peter was one of the first to leave his fishing nets and follow Jesus. He was the one who identified Jesus as the Christ, the Son of the Living God. Peter had been so strong that Jesus called him "Rock." He had been the one brave enough to dare to walk on water. Peter had been selected to go with Jesus to the Mount of Transfiguration and to the Garden of Gethsemane. He had vowed never to deny Jesus and had wept bitterly when he did. But Peter redeemed himself. He was one of the first disciples at the tomb, and he was selected to preach the sermon that signaled the birth of the church.

In what ways are you like Peter? Would you have asked Jesus to cure your mother-in-law? Would you have asked if you could walk on water? Could you have identified Jesus as the Christ? Would you have promised never to deny Jesus? Would you have broken that promise? Would you have regretted that denial? Could you have been the one to preach, signaling the beginning of the church? Just how much like Peter are you?

The second story I have chosen to highlight occurs after the death and resurrection of Jesus. It shows a Peter who is strong and committed to the church of Jesus Christ. Perhaps after we have experienced the risen Savior, we, too, will be strengthened. This story begins as Peter and John go to the temple at the hour of prayer. On the way, they encounter a man who has been lame from birth. He is begging for alms at the temple gate. The man asks Peter and John for money as they go by. But Peter responded to his request by asking the man to look at him. I believe that Peter had compassion for the man and perhaps wanted to see if the man truly wanted to be healed of his lameness. Once the man's eyes were fixed on Peter, Peter responded to the request. He let the man know that although he did not have silver or gold, what he had, he would give freely. He gave him the ability to get up and walk. Peter knew that if the man were no longer lame, he would not have to beg at the temple.

Sometimes we help those who beg by equipping them to help themselves. As the saying goes, they may need a helping hand, not a handout. Peter cared enough to give the beggar a helping hand. "And he took him by the right hand and raised him up; and immediately his feet and ankles were made strong" (Acts 3:7).

How often have you passed beggars without a thought of helping them? Do you consider telling them of a place where they might be able to find work? Do you offer them the opportunity to do some household chores for you? Do you tell them where a soup kitchen is? Or do you simply continue on your way, thankful that you are not one of the beggars?

The story of Peter's healing the lame beggar presents a strong postresurrection Peter. But I also remember the Peter who denied his Lord, and I believe that all of us are like Peter in many ways. He was both strong and weak, but he knew and loved his Lord. I count him as a strong man of compassion, and as I think about him, I wonder how many times we, like Peter, have denied our Lord. Some of the churches in Switzerland have roosters at the top of the cross on their churches. Christians there always want to remember that they have a tendency to deny in spite of their love for the Lord. Perhaps we all ought to wear a rooster right next to our crosses.

Lord, although I often experience Peter's weakness, I also want to experience his great faith. Help me be faithful enough to feed your lambs. Amen.

Luke

LUKE 1:1-4; 2 TIMOTHY 4:11

*P*aul called Luke "the beloved physician" in his letter to the Colossians (4:14). This term of endearment gives us some clue to Luke's capacity for compassion. He was a well-educated doctor, a historian, and a fine journalist. His unique Gospel and the book of Acts demonstrate his fine mastery of the Greek language. After investigating everything thoroughly, Luke tells us his intention is to write an orderly account of the events concerning Jesus that had been fulfilled (Luke 1:3-4). He wrote to the Greeks to convince them that Jesus was a priest sent from God to save them. He begins his Gospel with the story of the priest Zachariah, and the priestly theme is established.

Several themes of Luke's Gospel provide clues to the kind of man Luke was and the things that were important to him. Perhaps the first thing to note about Luke's depiction of Jesus is his concern to show the entire history of God's redemptive plan. Luke emphasizes that the events in the life of Jesus happened in fulfillment of the scriptures. God's plan for history and the redemption of creation can be seen through the works of God in Moses, the prophets, the ministries of John the Baptist and Jesus, and finally through the church (Acts). Thus, Luke's Gospel is the only one that begins with the story of the priest Zachariah and the birth of John the Baptist, the forerunner to Jesus.

A second important theme of Luke's Gospel is his message that through Jesus, God brings salvation for all. The radical inclusiveness of Jesus' ministry can be seen by the numerous stories Luke includes, stories in which Jesus reaches out to sinners, Samaritans, tax collectors, women, and outcasts. The social prejudices of the day would be radically reversed in the kingdom of God. Thus, Luke records with great compassion the visit of the angel Gabriel and the magnificent words that Mary and her cousin Elizabeth spoke. This is typical of Luke's writing, for he paid attention to what the women said and did. He also records the visit of the shepherds and the angels at the time of Jesus' birth. Luke wanted to make sure that the ordinary people were included in the telling of the Christmas story. Others had written about the visit and involvement of the kings.

In Luke's recording of the many parables of Jesus we see his compassion. He wants us to know that Jesus, being a good priest, came to save the lost. He tells us of the lost coin, the lost sheep, and the lost boy. As Luke records the parable of the Good Samaritan, he demonstrates the fact that all church people are not about the business of compassion. He never fails to include those special compassionate teachings of his Lord and Savior as he records the stories of the unjust judge and the Pharisee and the tax collector

Luke's account of the arrest and crucifixion of Jesus emphasizes the painful and tragic consequences of human sin. Jesus is betrayed, beaten, suffers, and is crucified for our sins. Luke wants us to feel Jesus' pain. *Have you ever told a story in such a way that you wanted people to feel the pain? Have you ever felt another's pain when listening to a person tell her or his story?* But even on the cross, Jesus gives a word of forgiveness to his executors and to the criminals crucified alongside him (23:34, 41-43). But God's plan of salvation is fulfilled even in the tragedy of the crucifixion; a thief, though guilty, is saved.

Luke makes sure that his writing includes Gentiles, as he was a non-Jew. He is an extraordinary evangelist who wants us to love and appreciate the ultimate priest. He was a companion of Paul and accompanied him on many of his missionary journeys as he sought to spread the word to all people. Much of the history of these journeys is recorded in his book of Acts of the Apostles. He was with Paul in Rome where he stayed with him during his final imprisonment. Paul writes in his second letter to Timothy, "Only Luke is with me" (2 Timothy 4:11a). Luke was not only compassionate, but also very loyal. *Could you hang in there during times of imprisonment? Do you have that much love and compassion?* Luke did.

Luke lets us all know that the Holy Spirit is always with us for comfort and hope, for he records the birth of the church and the coming of the Holy Comforter at Pentecost. What great hope his writing brings us! What a beloved and compassionate physician he was!

Lord, surround me with the wisdom, love, and evangelistic spirit of Luke. I want to serve you with great compassion. Amen.

Simeon

LUKE 2:25-34

Simeon is described as a righteous and devout man upon whom the spirit of God rested. Such a description is easily applied to one who, like Simeon, was compassionate. Simeon cared enough to spend the last years of his life looking forward to the "consolation of Israel," or the restoration of Israel with the promised coming of the Messiah. He wanted Israel to return to God and to its observance of God's laws. The Holy Spirit had revealed to Simeon that God would send one who would redeem his people. (The Holy Spirit during this time represented the truth that was revealed to men and women. It does not refer to the presence of God in the Trinity.) Simeon also knew through the Holy Spirit that he would not die until he had seen that redeemer. He waited patiently.

Simeon cared about the people of Israel. He cared enough to stay close to the temple so that he would be present when the Lord's Messiah, the Redeemer, appeared. The Spirit did not fail him, and he was led to the temple just at the time that Mary and Joseph brought Jesus to "do for him what was customary under the law" (Luke 2:27b). (The custom usually included the presentation of pigeons or doves.) Mary must have sensed Simeon's compassionate spirit, for she gave her baby to him. *How inclined would you have been to give your child to a stranger?* Remember, too, that babies do not easily go to people they do not know. Babies seem to sense something about the person who would hold them. The baby Jesus went to Simeon and seemed quietly to endure the song of praise that followed.

Simeon was overcome with emotion as he held the child and realized that he was holding the Lord's Messiah. He knew that his life was complete and that he could finally die in peace. He had lived to see the Lord's Messiah. He boldly proclaimed that Jesus was the means to salvation not only to the Jews, but to all people. He specifically noted that Jesus was "a light for revelation to the Gentiles" (Luke 2:32*a*). *How do you think Mary and Joseph responded to Simeon's pronouncements?*

But all that Simeon said was probably not music to Mary's ears. He told her that her son would be responsible for the falling and rising of many in Israel and that he would be opposed. These words alone would have given any mother reason for concern, but Simeon did not stop there. He continued by telling Mary that a sword would pierce her own soul, too (Luke 2:35). I can just imagine that Mary already felt the sword piercing her soul as she contemplated the destiny that awaited her son. To know of the great responsibility placed on one's child and to fear for that child's life does pierce a loving parent's soul. *Have you ever borne pain for a child charged with great responsibility and facing great opposition?*

Simeon's goal was realized. He lived to see the Lord's Messiah. He was a holy man who was guided by the Holy Spirit. He cared enough about his people to pray for their redemption and was rewarded by having the truth revealed to him. He was a strong man of compassion.

Lord, I not only want to see the Messiah, but also want the Messiah to be seen in me. Amen.

The Good Samaritan

LUKE 10:25-37

Using the story of the Good Samaritan, Jesus illustrated not only what it means to be a neighbor, but also what true strength and compassion are. Jesus began by describing the situation of a man who had been robbed, stripped, beaten, and left for dead on the road from Jerusalem to Jericho. Through this parable we come to understand just how much Jesus valued strength and compassion.

This parable teaches us that the so-called church people are often lacking in compassion. Both the priest and the Levite passed by the poor man but did not stop. Not only did they ignore the poor man, but also they took the extra precaution of crossing the street so that they would not pass by him on the same side of the street where he lay. They were the righteous people, the church people of today. They, like we, did and do not want to get involved. They did not bother to find out how badly hurt the man was. They did not even call 911, in today's terms. They did not act with neighborly compassion. *Would you have? Are you afraid to get involved?*

It took a foreigner, a Samaritan, who did not boast of or claim church or righteous connections, to show compassion.

What made the story even more shocking to Jesus' listeners was the relationship between Jews and Samaritans. There had been a long-standing hatred between these two peoples. Scholars believe that the Jews considered the Samaritans unclean people because they were descendants of Israelites who intermarried with the Assyrians after the fall of the Northern Kingdom (2 Kings 17:6, 24). In any case, it was clear that these two groups despised each other.

The Samaritan stopped, bandaged the victim's wounds, and provided what assistance he could. Then he put the man on his own animal and took him to a place where he could rest and be cared for. In today's terms, this stranger was not being so heavenly righteous that he was no earthly good. He cared. He stopped to bandage and treat the wounds. *Would we today? Are we too afraid of AIDS and infection?* Even doctors and trained medical personnel sometimes fail to render aid for fear of a lawsuit. But the Samaritan was not concerned that he was traveling and could be late for his appointment. He did not worry that he was using money that he needed to attend to his own affairs. He just did what he could for his neighbor. *Would you have been that generous with your time and money?*

Upon taking the victim to the inn, this compassionate Samaritan promised to return and repay the innkeeper for any additional expense. He did not do what he could and then leave, never to think about the man again, even though that is what many who might have stopped would have done. He promised to follow up and continue to be of compassionate assistance. The priest and the Levite did none of these things. Perhaps this parable actually defines men who are strong in heart and full of compassion. *What do you think?*

Holy God, if I have ever missed the opportunity to be a Good Samaritan, forgive me and help me be aware of and act upon the opportunities that present themselves in the future. Amen.

The Prodigal's Father

LUKE 15:11-32

M ost of us have heard this parable referred to as the story of the Prodigal Son, which emphasizes the younger son as the primary character in the story. According to this reading, the son's repentance of his sins and his return to his family are the main points of the parable. Although this is certainly an important dimension of the parable, the fact that Jesus tells this story following two other parables—the parable of the lost sheep and the lost coin—suggests that this is mainly a story about the rejoicing of the father over the restoration of his lost son.

In the character of the Prodigal's Father, we see the meaning of strength and compassion. This father extended unconditional love and compassion to his wayward son. Remember that this younger son had asked for his share of the inheritance to which he was entitled. Just the mere asking for something that is not yet rightfully yours might be cause for a father to withhold his love. But this was not so for the Prodigal's Father. He must have understood his son's longing to be independent, to make his own decisions, to see what he could accomplish without supervision. He wanted his son to be free. He did not want to demand that his son stay with him and wait until the inheritance would be given. The Prodigal's Father did what God has done for us. He gave the undeserving son his love and his blessings without any strings attached. The love he extended was unconditional. *What would you have done? Would you have believed your son was emotionally ready to handle his inheritance? Would you have attached conditions to what you gave?*

Like so many of us, the Prodigal Son was not mature enough to appreciate what his father had given him, so he squandered it in degenerate living. Desperate to find a way to sustain himself, the son accepted a job feeding the pigs of a Gentile farmer. Clearly, he had sunk about as low as he could. Not only was he starving without money to buy food, but also he was forced to take a job that no self-respecting Jew would have accepted since Jewish law forbade the raising of swine. Even worse, he found himself so hungry that he considered eating the very food that he fed to the pigs. In the depth of his despair, he realized that he needed to go back to his father and beg him to allow him to work as a servant. He knew that he deserved no better. He did not realize that some people will help you spend all that you have and then leave you when you are destitute. He did not expect his father to welcome him home, for he did not understand the strength and compassion his father possessed.

It is easy to imagine how the Prodigal's Father must have felt when he heard rumors of his son's dissolute lifestyle. He probably wondered where he had gone wrong and prayed that his son would come to realize the error of his ways. How like God he was! He probably never stopped hoping and praying that his son would come home. So when he saw his son in the distance, he recognized him instantly and prepared an elaborate celebration. Again, like God, he celebrated the homecoming of a sinner. *Could you have done that?*

This father did not hesitate to gather the finest clothes and jewels for his prodigal son. He did not even consider preparing a meager feast for the party. He wanted only the best because his son deserved the best. He did not remember his son's sins but was just thankful for his empty-handed return.

How many of us return to God empty-handed? How often have we squandered God's blessings and expected to be fully restored with no questions asked? Although God does not expect payment, have we even bothered to offer praise and thanksgiving for our blessings? Do you think the Prodigal Son offered that to his forgiving father? Would you have?

The Prodigal's Father was also called upon to forgive his elder son, who resented the fine treatment his wayward brother was receiving. We might identify with him also. *How often have we wondered why sinners seem to prosper while we who claim to be Christians often suffer?* Like the Prodigal's Father, God reminds us that God is always with us and will bring us through our suffering. God is always available to us for joyous worship and celebration.

Like the Prodigal's Father, God welcomes us with joy and forgiveness, though we are undeserving of such grace. Though God cares for those who have remained home and are faithful like the elder son, God desires the return of all who have lost their way. The return of even one lost person is cause for rejoicing and celebration.

The Prodigal's Father was compassionate and strong. He demonstrated what God is like.

Dear God, I am so grateful that you care for the lost and rejoice at the return of even one of your sheep. Your grace and mercy and forgiveness are gifts beyond all my deserving. Thank you! Amen.

One Cleansed Leper

❧

LUKE 17:11-19

*R*emembering to demonstrate thanksgiving is one element of compassion. One who is compassionate is appreciative of his or her blessings. Sometimes it takes great strength to prostrate oneself at another's feet and say thank-you, but this is just what One Cleansed Leper did.

Ten lepers approached Jesus on his way to Jerusalem. They must have heard about his great healing power, and although they were careful to keep their distance from him, they begged him for mercy. Jesus gave them simple instructions: "Go and show yourselves to the priests" (Luke 17:14). We know from other parts of the scripture that lepers were considered unclean and required by law to live outside the city (Numbers 5:2-3). And if a leper were fortunate enough to recover, he or she had to be certified as clean by a priest before returning to live in the city (Leviticus 14:23). Amazingly, the lepers followed Jesus' instructions, though they were not yet healed! While on their way to the priests, they were cleansed.

Just imagine what you might have done in their place. You are anxiously following the instructions you have been given. You do not doubt that you should follow these instructions because you know of the reputation of the man giving the instructions. On your way to the priests, you look at your hands and notice that they have been cleansed. *You are over-joyed, but what do you do? Do you continue on your way? Do you decide that it is no longer necessary to go to the priests as you had been instructed? Do you return to find Jesus and offer thanks? Do you think about praising God for your blessing?*

We don't know what the other nine did, but we do know that one cleansed leper did return, praised God, and pros-trated himself at Jesus' feet in gratitude. I believe that this man recognized the spirit of compassion so evident in Jesus and felt the need to show his own compassion through thanksgiving. Jesus asked him where the other nine were, but he could not answer. *Would you have tried to make excuses for the other nine?* Perhaps the cleansed leper felt badly that no one had accompanied him, but he could only thank Jesus and praise God for himself. A strong and com-passionate man always remembers to say thank you.

Lord, if I have forgotten to thank you for my many blessings, I pause to do that now. Thank you! Amen.

The Tax Collector

❧

LUKE 18:9-14

*J*esus gave us so many examples of compassionate men that I am convinced that being compassionate is a requirement of Christianity. In this particular example, Jesus warns us against self-righteousness.

A Pharisee and a tax collector went to the temple to pray. The Pharisee was so full of himself that he began to enumerate his virtues. He was self-righteous; he had no hint of compassion. Even though he claimed to obey the law, fast, and give his tithe, he did so as a matter of blind obedience. There was no spirit of humility or thanksgiving in his keeping the commandments. He was totally into himself. His concern was for his own righteousness. He did not care about others at all. In fact, he thought he was better than others.

A strong man of compassion is not like this Pharisee. He is not self-righteous. He does not blindly keep the commandments without true feeling and devotion to the one who has given the commandments. He is not concerned about his own welfare. He thinks about and cares for others. In fact he identifies with others and does not think that he is better. He understands that he is the least of all and unworthy of the great blessings that God bestows.

Think about the way you pray. *Do you enumerate your good works? Do you compare yourself to others? Do you sincerely pray for others? Do you express love and devotion for God? Do you express humility? Do you recognize your own unworthiness? Do you thank God for your many blessings? Do you ask for mercy? Are you like the Pharisee?*

By contrast, the tax collector was a man of compassion. He went to the temple lamenting his unrighteousness. He was so ashamed of being a sinner that he would not even look up to heaven. He did not even approach the holy areas of the temple, for he stood far off. He beat his breast in reproach for his sins. He knew he was a sinner in need of salvation and asked for God's mercy. He did not exalt himself or claim to be better than anyone else; he simply begged for mercy. He was humble, strong, and compassionate. Jesus described him as the type of man that went home justified. He is the one who would receive exaltation in heaven. *Will you?*

God, I recognize that I have sinned and fallen short of your glory. Forgive me and humble my heart to receive your salvation. Amen.

Zacchaeus

LUKE 19:1-10

Zacchaeus is described as a rich tax collector who was trying to see Jesus. He discovered that Jesus had come to Jericho, but a crowd of followers surrounded him. So, he went to the place where he expected Jesus to pass by, but others had gone to the same place. Zacchaeus was short, and he could not see Jesus through the crowd. So he ran ahead of the crowd and climbed a tree so that he would be able to see Jesus as he passed. He was willing to wait in the tree to see Jesus.

This seems like quite an ingenious move. I wonder whether many would have thought to climb a tree and how many would actually know how to climb a tree. Zacchaeus had to be more concerned about seeing Jesus than he was about how he looked climbing and waiting in a tree.

I imagine that Zacchaeus almost fell out of the tree when Jesus stopped just below him and told him to come down. I'll bet he was thinking, "Is he talking to me? Is he telling me that he is going home with me?" I am sure that when what Jesus said registered with Zacchaeus, he hurried to respond to Jesus' request. *Would you have been so quick to respond?*

Or would you have thought about all of the reasons for not wanting Jesus to come to your home?

Zacchaeus gives us the first glance at his compassion when he welcomes Jesus into his home. He obviously has the gift of hospitality, and one who has that gift is compassionate. Then Zacchaeus extends our brief glance at his compassionate spirit by telling Jesus that he will give half of his possessions to the poor and that he will pay back four times as much to anyone he has defrauded. One who does not have compassion is not concerned about the poor or about those whom he has defrauded. *Would you have been four times as concerned? Have you ever considered giving half of what you possess to the poor?*

The people in the crowd considered Zacchaeus to be a sinner. They were shocked that Jesus would even consider going to the home of such a man and began to grumble about Zacchaeus. In spite of their criticism, Zacchaeus demonstrated his faith and his compassionate spirit. I wonder how many in the crowd would have been as generous. *Would you? Would you have been concerned that the people in the crowd considered you a sinner? Would you have been discouraged or embarrassed by their talk?*

Zacchaeus was strong, brave, and resourceful. He found a way to overcome his short stature, and he boldly announced his intentions to provide for the poor and generously restore anything that he had wrongfully taken. As a man of compassion, he recognized his sins and sought salvation.

He was not disappointed, for Jesus said, "Today salvation has come to this house" (Luke 19:9*b*). Jesus came to seek out and save the lost. The compassionate Zacchaeus fit the description.

Holy God, like Zacchaeus, I want to see Jesus. I am prepared to repent of my sins and to welcome him into my home. Amen.

Andrew

JOHN 6:1-13

*A*lthough we first meet Andrew in the Gospel According to Matthew, I like this story in the book of John that gives us a hint of his compassionate spirit. We know that Andrew was one of the first disciples Jesus called. Andrew and his brother, Simon Peter, were working as fishermen. As Jesus passed by the Sea of Galilee, where they were casting their nets, he called them to follow him (Mark 1:16-18). Jesus told them that they would become fishers of people, and they did not hesitate to answer his call. *Isn't it interesting that Jesus called men who were working?*

Both Matthew and Mark record that Jesus called Peter and Andrew together. John, however, records that Andrew found Jesus while he was with John the Baptist, after he had been around Jesus for most of the day and had heard John call Jesus the "Lamb of God." Andrew went to get his brother and introduced him to Jesus (John 1:35-42). Andrew was so caring that he had to share the wonderful Messiah with his brother. He did not want his brother to miss out on the blessing that awaited. *When you have an encounter with Jesus, do you tell someone or try to introduce anyone to him? Or are you content to keep Jesus to yourself?*

The story in the scripture reference cited above is a

familiar one. It is the story of the feeding of the five thousand. This story is of special interest to me because Andrew is a key player. Andrew must have been mingling among the crowd and talking to the people to have discovered the boy with the five loaves and two fish. Andrew must have had a very warm and compassionate nature to convince the boy to share his lunch. Some people would have turned the boy off and caused him to hide whatever portion of his lunch he had remaining. (I can imagine that this was not the full lunch with which the boy had left home. What young boy would not have already eaten a portion of it? We know that it was getting late and that everyone was hungry.)

It seems that the boy willingly gave Andrew the uneaten portion of his lunch, and although Andrew was grateful to have found some food, he wondered what good so little would do among so many. Jesus asked Philip where they could buy food for the great crowd who had turned out to see his miracles and to hear him speak. Judging from Philip's response that it would take six-month's wages to buy food for that many people, he must have thought Jesus was crazy. But Jesus had a plan and gave simple instructions to have the crowd seated in an orderly fashion and blessed the loaves and fishes provided by the young boy. And miraculously there was enough for everyone present. So much in fact, that the disciples gathered the leftovers so that nothing was wasted.

What if Andrew had not taken the time to talk with the boy? What would Jesus have done about feeding so many? Andrew could not effect the miracle, but he could assist in providing what was needed. *How often do we simply give up when circumstances seem too overwhelming?* Perhaps a kind word or a friendly smile can provide the makings of a miracle. Andrew provided all of that. He was a man of compassion.

Lord, I want to be the one who introduces others to you. I want to be the friendly person who knows the children and assists in your miracles. I want to be like Andrew. Amen.

John

*T*he disciple John, son of Zebedee, is the one traditionally associated with the disciple simply referred to as the "beloved disciple" in the Gospel of John. John must have possessed a spirit of strength and compassion that caused Jesus to entrust his mother, Mary, to John's care as he hung from the cross. *Have you ever wondered why John was known as the beloved disciple? What about him was so loving? Why do you think Jesus chose him to provide for his mother? Don't those who are loving and those who are compassionate have the same characteristics?*

John and his brother James were among the first disciples called by Jesus. He was also a fisherman busily working when he was called. He was a part of Jesus' inner circle, always included when a small group was permitted to accompany Jesus. He was present at the transfiguration on the Mount and at Gethsemane. Along with Peter, he was chosen to help prepare the Lord's Supper (Luke 22:8). Jesus knew him well.

John was one of the few disciples still standing around the cross when Jesus was being crucified. Some of the women, including Mary, the mother of Jesus, were also there. I can just imagine that Jesus felt his mother's sorrow and knew that he would no longer be around in the flesh to care for her. He looked at those assembled and perhaps knew that John had the compassionate nature to care for his mother. With only a few words Jesus entrusted them each to the other: "'Woman here is your son.' Then he said to the disciple, 'Here is your mother.' And from that hour the disciple took her into his own home" (John 19:26b-27). Obviously John did not take the words of Jesus lightly, for he took Mary home with him. Why did Jesus not call on one of Mary's other children to care for their mother? The text simply doesn't tell us. We are told only that Jesus chose John, and John did not send her home with someone else; he took her home with him.

Although we do not know how long John remained at the cross, we do know that on the morning of the resurrection he was the first disciple to reach the empty tomb. When Mary Magdalene discovered that the body of Jesus was missing, she ran to tell Peter and John. Although both men set out running to the tomb, John reached there first. (Some believe that John was younger and the faster runner.) Seeing only linen wrappings, he did not go in. When Peter arrived, then he entered the tomb. Then John followed. Perhaps John felt so much love for Jesus that he could not bear facing the empty tomb alone. Discovering the empty tomb, both Peter and John went home, but Mary Magdalene stayed and was the first to see the risen Lord (John 20:1-18).

In his Gospel, John reveals his great desire for people to know and understand the nature of God by knowing and understanding Jesus. He tells us that Jesus was the living Word of God and that to know and understand Jesus is to know and understand God. He cares enough throughout his Gospel to use examples that are meaningful to his readers. He uses simple yet powerful metaphors such as bread, water, and light to describe the significance of Jesus to the world. We absolutely must have those things to live, just as it is through Jesus that we are given a more meaningful life. John calls Jesus the Good Shepherd, the door, the way, the truth, and the life. We relate to the shepherd who cares for his sheep; we know that we need a door to enter into life eternal, and we certainly need to know the truth and the way. Jesus is all of those. John cared enough to make it plain to those who would read and hear his Gospel as he recorded it.

Dear Jesus, would you choose me to care for your mother and to be your beloved disciple? I pray so. Amen.

Joseph of Arimathea

LUKE 23:50-56; JOHN 19:38-42

*A*ccording to most accounts, Joseph of Arimathea was a rich and powerful man. We are told in Luke and in Mark that he was a member of the Sanhedrin Council, which was the highest Jewish legislative body and whose members were the high priests. Matthew simply refers to Joseph as a disciple, and John tells us that he was a "secret disciple" of Jesus, perhaps indicating that he was afraid openly to show his allegiance to Jesus. He was simply and quietly waiting expectantly for the coming of the kingdom of God. Luke tells us that although Joseph was a member of the council, he did not take part in the arrest of Jesus and the decision to turn him over to the Roman authorities.

Though Joseph may have been afraid to speak up on Jesus' behalf at the trial or to show his allegiance publicly, he knew that he had to do something. Joseph felt so much compassion for this man who had taught of the kingdom of God and had healed the sick and performed many miracles that he felt compelled to go to Pilate and ask for Jesus' body. It was not unusual for a rich person to offer to pay for the burial of a beloved poor person, but it took real strength and compassion to provide a burial place for one whose murder had been demanded by the crowd and had caused such contro-versy. Joseph may have been afraid to admit to being a disci-ple, but he boldly provided for Jesus' body.

I wonder what Pilate thought when Joseph asked for the body. *Did Pilate recall the warning his wife had sent him about the man called Jesus? Was Pilate afraid to deny the body to this rich man? Did Pilate think that Joseph, as a member of the Sanhedrin, could quietly take the body away? Did he think that the disciples of Jesus might stir the Jews to violence if permission to remove the body was granted?* Perhaps all of these thoughts passed through Pilate's mind once it was time to remove the body.

I believe that it was because Joseph really loved Jesus that he decided to do what he could to restore some dignity to an unjust and horrible situation. I believe that Joseph regretted not speak-ing up at the council meeting and that he wondered whether his voice and vote could have made a difference. All that was left for him to do was to offer a new, unused tomb. Perhaps it was a tomb he had purchased for his own use. The accounts seem to vary with regard to this point, but at any rate it was a clean place in which the body could lie until it was properly prepared. Joseph lovingly wrapped the body, placed it in the tomb, and rolled a stone in front of the opening to seal it. It was a peace-ful resting place for the Prince of Peace. Perhaps Joseph knew that Jesus would not need the tomb for very long. *After all, hadn't Jesus said that he would rise in three days?*

Joseph of Arimathea was a rich and compassionate man. How strange it is that those two words, "rich" and "compas-sionate," seem to be incompatible when used together. *Do you know any rich and compassionate people?* We may believe that rich people are rarely compassionate, but Joseph was. That is why I consider him to be a strong man of compassion.

Lord, sometimes I am afraid to speak up and witness for you. Take away my fear and increase my willingness to share my possessions. Amen.

Stephen

❧

ACTS 6–7

*S*tephen was a Greek-speaking Jew known as a Hellenist, and he became one of the earliest Christians in Jerusalem, as well as the first Christian martyr. We have to search long and hard to find a stronger, more compassionate man than Stephen. He was among the seven chosen by the disciples to distribute food to the widows who were being neglected. These seven were chosen because they were "full of the Spirit and of wisdom" and would make strong leaders of the community. The disciples felt comfortable turning this task over to them so that their own time could be spent in "prayer and . . . serving the word" (Acts 6:3-4). Surely the disciples also recognized the compassionate spirit of Stephen and the others, and they had them stand before the apostles, "who prayed and laid their hands on them" (Acts 6:6).

Stephen was "full of grace and power" and did "great wonders and signs among the people" (Acts 6:8). We know that he was full of compassion because he was able to accomplish so much. It was obvious that God was with him and his role as a leader in the community expanded. When some men from the synagogue of the Freedmen, or the synagogue of emancipated Jews or their descendants, tried to argue with him, they failed because of his wisdom and conviction. But because of their jealousy, they manufactured charges against him and brought him before the council. He was accused of blasphemy and of trying to overturn the laws of Moses. Even as Stephen listened to the false witnesses and charges against him, those present at the council noticed that his "face was like the face of an angel" (Acts 6:15). *Could that have been said about you if you were listening to someone telling lies about you?* Even as he was being falsely accused, Stephen's spirit was angelic and compassionate.

Stephen eloquently responded to their charges by reviewing the history of Israel and God's liberation of and covenant with the people of Israel. But the people had sinned and turned against God, ignoring the prophets and murdering the Messiah. Stephen ended his speech by suggesting that it was his accusers, not him, who had turned away from God and not kept the law. Of course, his accusers were enraged not only by this, but also by Stephen's proclamation that he saw a vision of the heavens opening and the Son of Man standing at the right hand of God (Acts 7:56). Knowing that they were not listening to him, Stephen prayed that Jesus would receive his spirit and that what his murderers were doing would not be held against them. In response, they dragged Stephen outside and began to stone him.

Even in the midst of such distress, Stephen was concerned about those who were killing him. He prayed that they would be forgiven just as Jesus had prayed for those who killed him. *Could you have uttered such a prayer?* Stephen was strong in heart. He was eloquent in the face of false accusations. He stood alone when he was accused and denied neither his faith nor his compassion for the children of God.

Dear Jesus, Stephen used your example and gave his life while forgiving his murderers. I may not have to give my life, but help me forgive those who accuse me. I pray that my accusers are accusing me of living for you. Amen.

The Ethiopian Eunuch

ACTS 8:26-40

*T*he Ethiopian Eunuch, a court official of the queen of the Ethiopians, was returning home from worship in Jerusalem. As he rode along in his chariot, he read aloud from the prophet Isaiah. He did not know that God would direct Philip to join him, but when Philip approached and asked if he knew what he was reading, he replied, "How can I, unless someone guides me?" (Acts 8:31*a*). His response makes us aware that the eunuch had a teachable and humble spirit, and he invited Philip to join him.

Perhaps this eunuch wanted company as he continued on his journey. Perhaps he felt compassion for Philip, who was on foot, and he wanted to offer him a ride. Perhaps he really did not understand what he was reading and felt that Philip could help him. We don't know what motivated the eunuch to invite Philip to join him, but we know that he did and that he appears to have wanted guidance. *Which explanation seems most reasonable to you?*

The scripture he was reading described a silent lamb brought to the shearer, denied justice and life on earth. The eunuch was moved by this passage and asked to whom it referred. His question provided Philip the opportunity to tell him about Jesus. Philip did not rush through his witness; he started with the scripture and proclaimed the good news. If the eunuch had not felt compassion for the one to whom the scripture referred or identified with being an outcast or outsider as both a Gentile and a eunuch, he would not have asked the question that led to his salvation. *How might you have answered the eunuch's question? Do you believe your answer would have led to the eunuch's salvation? Have you ever led anyone to salvation?*

The eunuch's questions did not end with the one to whom the scripture referred; for after hearing the good news about Jesus and seeing water along the road, he asked another question: "What is to prevent me from being baptized?" (Acts 8:37b). The eunuch was not only passionate about Jesus; he was also passionate about becoming a follower. After being baptized, he continued on his way rejoicing.

The Ethiopian Eunuch was open to information; he was curious about and concerned for one who had been murdered and humiliated. He wanted to join that little band of Christians who could so passionately explain the scriptures and proclaim the good news. He was able to rejoice because he had received salvation. He would not have been saved if he had not been strong and compassionate.

Lord, I want to know more and more about you. I want to be evangelistic as I receive the word of salvation. Help me be a witness to others in both word and deed so that they, too, might believe. Amen.

The Jailer

ACTS 16:25-40

Paul and Silas had cast a spirit of divination out of a slave girl. The girl's fortune-telling had brought a good deal of money to the girl's owners, so her owners were angry that Paul and Silas had deprived them of this source of income. They had Paul and Silas dragged to the marketplace and charged with disturbing the city and advocating Jewish customs that were not lawful for Romans. The crowd joined in the accusations, and Paul and Silas were stripped, beaten, and thrown into jail. The jailer was given strict orders to see that they were securely bound. "Following these instructions, he [the jailer] put them in the innermost cell and fastened their feet in the stocks" (Acts 16:24). The jailer went to sleep, believing there was no way his prisoners could escape.

Paul and Silas were not deterred by their confinement. They spent the evening singing hymns and praying to God; and at about midnight, a violent earthquake shook the foundations of the prison, opening all the doors and loosening the prisoners' chains. The prisoners were free to go, but they remained, continuing to listen to the singing and praying of Paul and Silas. Startled awake by the noise, the jailer ran to the prison and saw that the doors stood wide open. He assumed that all of the prisoners were free and drew his sword to kill himself. Perhaps he knew that the authorities would kill him for he had been given strict orders to keep the prisoners guarded. But Paul told him not to harm himself, because they were all still there. *Can you imagine the feelings the jailer must have experienced?* Surely he wondered what kind of religion kept free men in a jail, and what kind of men continued to sing and pray to a God who had made a miraculous way of escape for them. *Why hadn't they left? And were they actually concerned for his life?*

Whatever the religion was that Paul and Silas were practicing, the jailer knew that he needed it. He asked, "Sirs, what must I do to be saved?" (Acts 16:30b). He was told to believe in the Lord Jesus and he and his whole household would have salvation. Then he and his household listened to the word of the Lord. The next act that the jailer performed caused me to consider him a strong man of compassion. He washed Paul's and Silas's wounds, saw to it that he and his family were baptized, and then fed Paul and Silas. There was great rejoicing because he had become a believer in God. *Would you have sought salvation in this situation? Would you have wanted your family to be saved as well? Would you have washed and fed the men you had jailed? Would you have been as compassionate as the jailer was?*

The jailer also understood that Paul and Silas did not want to be quietly released. When the magistrates heard what had occurred during the night, they wanted Paul and Silas to leave in secret. But Paul and Silas told the jailer that they had been publicly jailed and they wanted to be publicly released. The jailer understood that they were Roman citizens who had done no wrong. The jailer sent the message to the magistrates who came to apologize and release the prisoners. The jailer must have been pleased that those who had brought salvation to his household were innocent of all wrongdoing and were released in a public manner. They

were free to return to Lydia's house where they had established a church. After encouraging the new Christians there,
they left town. Surely the jailer's kindnesses to Paul and Silas
demonstrated that he was a man of compassion.

*Lord, I know the jailer must have wondered what manner of
man could inspire freed men to remain bound. I know that
manner of man, and I strive to be just like him. I am free,
but I choose to be bound by the Word. Amen.*

Paul

ROMANS 16:1-16; PHILEMON

You might remember that Paul, known as Saul, persecuted Christians before his conversion. He had stood by and
watched as Stephen was stoned. *How could he possibly be a
strong man of compassion?* The answer lies in the power of
God to save. Salvation causes one to think and act differ-
ently. Salvation instills compassion, and Paul had his
Damascus experience: he had met Jesus and had been saved.

There are two particular acts of Paul's compassion to
which I will direct you. They are especially meaningful to me
as a woman and as one whose ancestors were slaves. The
first involves Phoebe, a deacon and perhaps the pastor of the
church at Cenchreae. Contrary to popular opinion, Paul
applauded her efforts on behalf of the church. He wrote to
the church at Rome that she should be welcomed in the Lord
"as is fitting for the saints." He further instructed the church
to help her in any way required because she had been a benefactor of many, including him (Romans 16:1-2).

We really don't know much more about Phoebe. Clearly,
she was a leader in the church and also probably a woman
of some means (to be a benefactor). Many have suggested
that Phoebe was, in fact, the bearer of Paul's letter to the

Roman church. *Why was Paul so concerned about Phoebe and the way she would be received? Were women ministers shunned? Was it hard for women to receive the type of welcome extended to men? Did Paul know something about the leaders in the church at Rome?* We might compare this part of Paul's letter to one that might be written by a bishop or district superintendent in The United Methodist Church. *Is it necessary to ask a church to welcome a woman minister in a way befitting a saint? Is it necessary to tell of her past work and accomplishments for the Lord?* Perhaps it is. At any rate Paul knew that as Phoebe traveled to Rome, she needed a kind word of recommendation and encouragement from him, and he provided it. He had compassion for her and for her ministry.

Another instance of Paul's compassion can be found in his letter to Philemon. Paul writes on behalf of Onesimus, Philemon's slave, who had escaped and had met Paul in prison. Paul urged Philemon to take Onesimus back "no longer as a slave but more than a slave, a beloved brother" (Philemon 16). While Onesimus had been with Paul, he had become a Christian convert. I am sure that Philemon contemplated this request for quite a while. Onesimus had escaped. He was a runaway slave who might have even stolen from his master. He had met Paul and had been converted. *Did this mean that any slave claiming to be converted should be freed? How would his other slaves feel about Onesimus if he were welcomed as a brother? Would Onesimus's freed status cause chaos among the other slaves? Why was Paul so concerned about this one slave?*

Paul's warm greeting and praise must have comforted Philemon as he read the first part of his letter. Paul let him know how much his love for all of the saints had encouraged him. Then Paul told him that he could order him to receive Onesimus as a freed man but instead appealed to Philemon on the basis of love and the spirit of forgiveness. He further told Philemon how much Onesimus had come to mean to him while he was imprisoned and how helpful he could still be to both of them. Paul promised to repay anything that Onesimus might owe, for he had great love for him and wanted there to be nothing to keep Onesimus and Philemon from complete harmony. Paul was confident that Philemon would do even more than he asked. He closed his letter with a request that a room also be prepared for him.

Paul was a strong and brave man. He was confident of the love and faith of all of the saints. He believed in the conversion of all who listened to and received the Word of God. He wanted every Christian to receive every other Christian as a beloved brother. He was clear that through Christ, the normal relationships of the world were changed and transformed. *Would you have been that confident? What would you have done in Philemon's place? How do you think Onesimus felt? Would you have been afraid to return to the home of your former owner?*

Paul expected and required Christian obedience in all areas of life. He felt compassion for Onesimus and he felt compassion for Philemon. He knew they both would do the right thing. Paul was strong in heart.

Lord, I pray for Paul's missionary spirit, his knowledge of the Word, his zeal for writing and preaching, and his absolute devotion to you. Amen.

Jesus

MATTHEW 5

*T*he ultimate strong man of compassion is Jesus. We could look at each strong man of compassion that we have considered and discover that wherever an element of compassion was shown, Jesus showed that element even more. Where there was sharing, Jesus shared. Where there was weeping, Jesus wept. Where there was sacrificing, Jesus sacrificed. Where there was prayer, Jesus prayed. No matter what strength, what element of compassion, Jesus demonstrated them all. But Jesus represents more than simply the best example of the strong, compassionate man—he *defines* true strength and compassion. The world expected a Messiah that would come with strength and power to defeat Israel's oppressors and restore the kingdom of Israel to its former glory. Instead, Jesus was the suffering Messiah, who paradoxically demonstrated his power by his willingness to lay down his life for the sins of the world.

As Christians, we, too, are called to follow Jesus' example, to be people of love and compassion, of sacrifice and service. *But just what does that look like? What are the qualities and marks of compassion that we should strive for?* I believe that Jesus' teachings found in the Sermon on the

Mount help provide a good definition of a compassionate Christian. Let's look at some of those qualities listed in the Beatitudes.

Each of the Beatitudes begins with the word "blessed." In the Greek, this word is used to describe the gods, so "blessed" implies a godlike joy or a godlike happiness. We know that our God is a compassionate God, and if it is possible for us to experience joy or happiness by doing those things that make us blessed, then we certainly ought to try.

What is the first thing we can do to be compassionate and subsequently blessed? We can be poor in spirit or realize our own helplessness. One who is poor in spirit puts his or her complete trust in God. One's identity and security are found in God alone. Such a person is detached from the things of the world so that he or she may be attached to God. That person is truly compassionate and can look forward to the reward of the kingdom of heaven. When we look to Jesus, we see that he put his complete trust in God and was obedient even to his death on the cross. He could have trusted in himself and come down off that cross, but he trusted God and reigns with God in the kingdom. He let the light of his compassionate spirit shine, and his Father was glorified. *What kind of light are you shining?*

The compassionate person who mourns—one who sincerely mourns, mourns for the whole world and for all of its suffering—will be comforted. That person also mourns for his or her own sin and suffering; yet, because one is willing to offer a broken and contrite heart, he or she can be comforted by God's great love. Jesus wept, and he experienced that godlike joy as he was comforted. *What causes you to mourn? Do you ever feel blessed through your mourning? Do you feel that your capacity for compassion is enhanced?*

The meek are also blessed because they are controlled by God. The meek are humble enough to know that God is in control of their lives. The meek do not try to control others, for they concentrate on letting God control them. Jesus prayed that God's will, not his, would be done, and Jesus inherited the earth. He is the King of kings. *Who controls you? Do you ever feel in complete control? Do you have enough compassion to allow God to control you?*

We are blessed and experience godlike joy when we hunger and thirst for righteousness. We have to want goodness desperately to prevail in the world. Hungering and thirsting for righteousness is automatically a part of our compassionate nature. We cannot want only partial goodness; we have to want it all. We often make the mistake of thinking righteousness simply means not committing a sinful act. Jesus let us know that even thinking about the act is sin. We have to want total righteousness and strive to live in the blameless and compassionate way that Jesus did. It is only then that we can be satisfied. *Do you hunger and thirst for righteousness like a person who has not eaten or drunk for days? Is this hunger and thirst a natural part of who you really are?*

We experience godlike joy and blessedness when we are merciful. One has to be compassionate to be merciful. In order to give and receive mercy, we have to do what God did in Jesus Christ. God got inside our skin and became human in Jesus. Through this act, God could grant us mercy because God could see with our eyes and feel with our hearts and think with our minds. If we are to be merciful to others, we must use all of our compassion to empathize with them. God showed us that we could not show mercy to others without truly getting inside their lives. Only through the grace and mercy granted to us by God through Jesus Christ are we enabled in turn to grant mercy to others, to truly get inside their skin. *What do you have to do to equip yourself to grant and receive mercy? With whom do you need to empathize? Are you compassionate enough to do it?*

We are blessed and experience godlike happiness when we become pure in heart like little children who truly see God. Oh what joy awaits us when we become pure in heart.

We, like Jesus, see God and know that we are united with God. Let children provide an example as you remember that Jesus said that unless we become like little children, we cannot enter the kingdom of heaven. *Are you pure in heart? Do children love you? Do children recognize your loving and compassionate nature? Do you expect to see God?*

Jesus brought peace, not a sword. Peacemakers will be called the children of God. Peacemakers are compassionate and strong. They do not just avoid conflict; they actively work for peace. Jesus was a peacemaker, and he was the Son of God. If we also want to be children of God, we must work for peace and reconciliation. *Are you a peacemaker, or does trouble follow wherever you go? Do you actively work to bring peace to the situations in which you are involved?*

Jesus was persecuted for righteousness' sake. He was reviled and persecuted and all manner of evil was uttered against him falsely, but his reward is great in heaven. We, too, must look forward to being reviled and persecuted if we want that great reward. *Does anyone ever speak falsely against you? Do you ever feel reviled and persecuted?* If not, perhaps your reward does not await you in heaven. If so, rejoice and be exceedingly glad. Be assured that others have noticed your compassionate spirit and have sought to accuse you falsely. If this is so, you are living just as Jesus taught.

Strong and compassionate men have the prime example in Jesus, and he has given us the formula in the Sermon on the Mount. *Can you live up to the description?* Every man discussed in these chapters had one or more of these qualities. Jesus exemplified all of them. He was and is the strongest in heart, the Man of compassion. I praise God for Jesus, and I pray that you and I will strive to be like him.

Dear Jesus, thank you for the gospel. Thank you for salvation. Thank you for being Emmanuel, God with us. Amen.

*B*ibliography

Barclay, William. *The Gospel of Matthew*, vols. 1 and 2. Philadelphia: Westminster Press, 1975.

Barker, William P. *Everyone in the Bible*. Westwood, N.J.: Fleming H. Revell Company, 1966.

Halley, Henry H. *Bible Handbook*. Chicago: Henry H. Halley, 1959.

Kimbrough, Marjorie L. *She Is Worthy*. Nashville: Abingdon Press, 1994.

———. *Stories Between the Testaments*. Nashville: Abingdon Press, 2000.

The New Oxford Annotated Bible. New York: Oxford University Press, 1991.

The Spiritual Formation Bible. Grand Rapids, Mich.: Zondervan Publishing House, 1999.